FROM
ACHILLES
TO CHRIST

The Myth of the Hero
in Tolstoy's War and Peace

FROM
ACHILLES
TO CHRIST

The Myth of the Hero
in Tolstoy's War and Peace

By Laura Jepsen

International Standard Book Number: 0-9602082-1-6
Library of Congress Number: 78-70416

Printed in U.S.A.

SESQUICENTENNIAL EDITION

Commemorating the 150th Anniversary
of the Birth of
Leo Tolstoy

September 1828–September 1978

FOREWORD

SHARING a conviction of Northrop Frye, that "the study of mediocre works of art remains a random and peripheral form of critical experience, whereas the profound masterpiece draws us to a point at which we seem to see an enormous number of converging patterns of significance," I set out to discover such patterns in epic genre, in Homer's *Iliad* and Tolstoy's *War and Peace*.

Regarding myth as the matrix of epic, I have attempted to show how myth defines in Homeric and Christian traditions the religious beliefs, historical assumptions, and cosmological speculations perceptible in works which differ more chronologically than thematically and structurally. Like Homer, Tolstoy uses the ancient symbols of myth and metaphor, but he pours into those old skins the new wine of his own age.

The key to the mythical method lies not solely in the use of ancient mythology, but, as T. S. Eliot has enunciated, in "manipulating a continuous parallel between contemporaneity and antiquity." In pursuing this method Tolstoy adopts a means of rising above the exigencies of his time and imparts to epic genre the norms of an archetypal age.

From Achilles to Christ, the myth interpreting the significance of the short-lived, semi-divine hero has been perpetuated. What, then, do the heroes of *War and Peace* have in common with the Homeric heroes? Counterpointing of main characters from the two traditions reveals an underlying archetypal pattern of human experience. Archetypal patterns multiplied relate the present to the past,

Tolstoy's Moscow to Homer's Ilium, our diversity to our uniformity, and ultimately reconcile our individuality with our humanity.

Ultimately, in the enunciation of a doctrine peculiarly his own, Tolstoy transmutes the orthodoxy developed by the church into a philosophy akin to the teachings of early Christianity. Embodying that philosophy, yet evolving from the ancient archetypal pattern of the epic hero, a new pattern emerges, an antitype, albeit one indebted in origin to the earlier counterpart.

Although contemporary analogies with Greek myths assert indebtedness to the past, it can hardly be denied that in the Western world the Christian myth is often regarded as more authoritative than the pagan. Thus, the myth of the first woman, Eve, in the Christian tradition has a canonical position superior to that of the mythical first woman, Pandora. Similarly, to explain the repeopling of the earth after a flood, the myth of Noah's Ark, whether we believe in its historicity or not, holds a position superior to the parallel myth of the Greek progenitors, Pyrrha and Deucalion.

Since the grammar of myth is metaphor, we can again observe the parallel import in similar metaphorical clusters, as, for example, in those surrounding the metaphorical apple. In the classical tradition the Apple of Discord tossed into the wedding feast of Peleus and Thetis, parents of Achilles (and thus ironically engendering the death of their son), results in the death of Hector and the consequent fall of Troy. To the apple in the Biblical Garden of Eden may be traced the fall of Adam, followed by the historical parallel, the fall of Israel, and, according to Biblical tradition, the fall of Man. In both instances the fall of an individual is followed by the fall of a nation, though in the Christian tradition the myth may explain a "fortunate fall."

Further illustrations appear in the body of the book, where, observing the dictum of Callimachus, that a big book is a great error (a big bore),[1]

Μέγα βιβλίον, μέγα κακόν,

I have attempted to be brief.

To all who have aided in the preparation of this book I give grateful acknowledgement, especially to Professor Paul Debreczeny, of the University of North Carolina, and to Professor T. Walter Herbert, of the University of Florida.

Laura Jepsen
Tallahassee, Florida
September 1978

CONTENTS

NOTES

INDEX

FROM
ACHILLES
TO CHRIST

The Myth of the Hero
in Tolstoy's War and Peace

Myth

Chapter I

MYTH AS MATRIX OF EPIC

THE EMERGENCE from myth of Homeric and Christian traditions demonstrates the inseparable association of myth and literature. Since myths are believed to have happened, they are highly significant in explaining certain anthropological aspects of literature. The emergence of epic from Homeric and Christian traditions demonstrates the partial emancipation of epic genre from its mythical origin, but perhaps more significantly it reveals the fact that epic form and myth cannot be completely dissociated. In a wider sense, it poses the question as to whether any literary form can be created without reference to its origin in myth. Because man has recourse to myth as the appropriate approach to certain baffling aspects of experience, myth becomes the matrix of literature.

Though the chronicler of history may rightly be skeptical, the writer of intellectual history can hardly ignore the fact that because the singer and the audience regarded myths as historical, they were deeply influential in molding the thought and action of their time. In the Homeric epic we trace the influence of myth which is doubtless the echo of historical events—events which by long preservation in the mind of posterity have reached heroic magnitude.

If history is defined as an explanation of the life of man through the literature which represents his highest ideals, then in the guise of history, epic poetry fulfills another function, that of instruction. Indeed, the oral epic spread the wisdom of the Achaeans long before Homer became the educator of Hellas. It is likely that the *Iliad* and the *Odyssey* were first sung by wandering rhapsodes at the manors of the nobility. Thus the memory of the past enshrined in epic poetry became in ancient Hellas an exhortation to present action. Homer's epics, cherished early for their praise of illustrious ancestors, later taught as textbooks to the young, sung by rhapsodes at the Panathenaic festival, were highly influential in shaping the culture of Athens.

The connection of myth with epic arises from the association of epic with the old heroic lay, in which the rhapsode praises all that is praiseworthy in the world. He sings of the glorious past—for traditions of the past are comprised of glory, of deeds of great men and of extraordinary events. Such are the κλέα ἀνδρῶν (IX, 189), the glorious deeds of men, which Achilles celebrates in his hut while Patroclus listens for the conclusion. Such are the heroic lays sung by the rhapsodes in the *Odyssey*. We may suppose that Homer is describing in the *Odyssey* singers of his own time: Phemius (speaker of fame) who chants, much to Penelope's distress, of the woeful return of the Achaeans from Troy (I, 325–359) and Demodocus (a name alluding to the publicity he creates)[1] who sings at the court of Alcinous of the quarrel between Achilles and Odysseus (VIII, 72–84).[2]

Since the singer was more than an entertainer, he was honored as a mentor from whom men learned not only the history of the past but also the moral wisdom of a nation. Moreover, his words carried more than human authority. The ancient Greek regarded the singer, *aidos*, as divinely inspired, his song breathed into him by the muses. Hence

6

the invocation at the beginning of the *Iliad*, "Sing, O Muse!" The entreaty is repeated whenever inspiration flags. The singers Homer portrays in the *Odyssey* are highly regarded for they serve as an intermediary between the world of the spirit and the world of man.[3]

One is disposed to ask whence come these heroic lays, the subject of the rhapsode's song. Assuming that Homer inherited a secularized tradition, that is one in which the god of the ritual had become emancipated from the myth which had interpreted that ritual, we can understand how the mythical story of the god might become the adventure story of the hero, a story in which it is possible to include both historical persons and historical events in epic form. As the field of epic widened, conflict with symbols of death might become war against human enemies. Epic thus becomes an account of the hero's glorious deeds.[4] It seems, then, that behind the epic lies the heroic lay and behind the lay the myth and behind the myth the ritual which has its origin in nature.

In Homer we detect traces of primitive man's way of recognizing his dependence on the powers of nature. Initially nature is the universal mother, the creative force, a daimon neither good nor evil. From her comes man's strength, as the myth of Hercules and Antaeus illustrates. According to the myth, the semi-divine Hercules, performing one of his celebrated exploits, overthrew the giant Antaeus, son of the Earth Mother, from whom he derived his strength. Antaeus was invincible so long as he remained in contact with the earth. One after another, strangers coming to this country wrestled with him, were overthrown, and subsequently put to death. Hercules encountering the giant found it of no avail to persist in trying to throw him, for he always rose with renewed strength from the earth. Hence the wily Hercules lifted Antaeus from the source of his strength, the earth, and strangled him in the air.

Primitive man not only personified the earth but also regarded aspects of the earth, the tree and the rock, as alive. Why should he not expect them to feel with him— to be troubled by like passions as his own? The phrase "from oak tree or from rock," which occurs in the *Iliad* (XXII, 126) when Hector pauses in his flight and resolves to confront Achilles, recurs a number of times in Greek literature and appears to be a phrase from an old folk tale dealing with the origin of mankind from trees or rocks. The phrase occurs also in the *Odyssey*, where Penelope, pressing Odysseus to reveal his identity, urges her compassion: not from oak tree nor from rock does she take her origin:[5]

οὐ γὰρ ἀπὸ δρυός ἐσσι παλαιφάτου οὐδ' ἀπὸ πέτρης.

Odyssey (XIX, 163)

Nature has her own laws; she is a cosmos, an order, a harmony of nature, with a way of justice (*dike*) of her own. Sowing the seed and tending it in spring represents man's desire to assist the rebirth of the dead plant world each year. The annual death and revival of vegetation augurs a corresponding hope of generic rebirth. Transformed into a ritual, the rebirth of the seed into a new plant symbolizes the hope of human immortality.

Ritual is customarily associated with the transition from life to death and then again to life, for death is necessary to renewal of life and must be experienced at least symbolically before life is possible. Myth tells the story of this process, thus accounting for ritual.

Perhaps no analogy is more deeply rooted in man's thought than that which likens the laws of man to the processes of nature. It is the first law of mankind, the knowledge of which is made available to him by the spectacle and even more by the experience of life's vicissitudes, that, in conformity with nature, all men are subject to the universal pattern of birth, decay, and death. This pattern which nature demonstrates shapes the direction of man's thought and in time becomes a fruitful source of poetical expression.

Eventually primitive man stands apart and views nature as a separate order. Then he speaks of sympathy with nature, in which he finds a link with cosmic events. In the cosmic rhythm he finds a pattern for human life. The vegetation rites that bring sustenance to mankind now become the symbols of the cycle of birth, death, and renewal —Homer's generation of leaves and Price Andrew's leafing oak.

Perhaps no analogy is more fertile in man's mind than that which likens life to the rhythm of nature, the ever recurring cycle of the seasons. To Homer it yielded one of his most characteristic similes, that of the comparison of the generations of leaves to the generations of men (VI, 145–149). "Even as are the generations of leaves such are those likewise of men; the leaves that be the wind scattereth on the earth, and the forest buddeth and putteth forth more again, when the season of spring is at hand; so of the generations of men one putteth forth and another ceaseth." The same thought is expressed by Apollo in a simile comparing men to dying leaves, "pitiful mortals, who like unto leaves now live in glowing life, consuming the fruit of the earth, and now again pine unto death" (XXI, 464–466).

The deep concern of epic poetry with mortality and immortality seems to have sprung from the prehistoric past, a time in which the myth enacted as a ritual ceremony, possibly in an effort to overcome death, eventually became the epic of oral tradition. The ritual enactment of an event symbolizing the alternation of opposites in nature —the sun and the moon, the day and the night, the recurring seasons marked by equinoxes and solstices, and the revolving years—expresses a principle underlying all life on earth. Eventually the annual triumph in nature of life over death, of order over chaos, of good over evil, gave birth to the mystery religions, of which Christianity is heir. Tolstoy's Christian heroes are indebted to an ancient heritage.

Homer, like Tolstoy, is constantly aware of the manifold vicissitudes of nature that are the parent of perplexity. Like Tolstoy, Homer is occupied by the thought of change, how the ancient city must fall, and fall too must the conquerors, but Homer offers little comfort in the hereafter for his fallen warriors. In the *Iliad* we see the phantom of Patroclus seeking burial in order that he may find rest in a nebulous Hades (XXIII, 69–107) and in the *Odyssey*, where Homer pictures a geographical hereafter, we learn that Achilles would rather be a slave on earth than king in the other world (XI, 489–491). For Tolstoy, however, heir to the Christian tradition, the story of the dying and resurrected god has given birth to a new myth which promises salvation in the life to come. As Christ rose from the dead, so Tolstoy's Christian heroes triumph over death.

Since we have been referring to the poetry of Homer as though Homer were the author of both the *Iliad* and the *Odyssey* (though the *Odyssey* seems to depict a more advanced, hence later, civilization), it might be well to consider the pedigree and the date of the legendary singer of Ionia. The first ancient author to refer to both the *Iliad* and the *Odyssey* by name as works of Homer was Herodotus, nephew of an epic poet.[6] As to Homer's era, Herodotus tells us that Homer lived not more than four hundred years before his own time, and Thucydides says only that Homer lived long after the Trojan War. As focal points, the date about 850 B.C. for Homer and about 1200 B.C. for the Trojan War may suffice.[7]

Greene suggests that Hesiod in his "Myth of the Ages," revealing the cosmic degeneration of man, may be paying tribute to Homer when he interrupts his scheme by introducing an Age of Heroes.[8] Moreover, they could point to the testimony of Hesiod, who in his record of the ages of man places between the age of bronze and the age of iron an age of heroes who fought at Thebes and at Troy. The men Homer had called heroes the Greeks of the sixth and fifth centuries B.C. honored as their ancestors. They regarded them as a generation of superior beings who sought and deserved honor.

That the *Iliad* and the *Odyssey* are the result of a long evolution in oral tradition is commonly accepted. The association of Homer with oral tradition becomes clearer when we recall that ancient singers expressed in lament the fame of the dead and in panegyric the praise of the living, the chief ends of heroic lays. Through the heroic

11

lay the function of genre is developed while its original aim is retained, to connect man with the unseen forces of the world beyond.

Though the Homeric epic belongs to a tradition in which poems were improvised, some time or other they were written down, and, according to Bowra, it is likely that they were recorded in the Poet's lifetime.[9] Yet even if writing existed in Homer's time, it is doubtful that Homer relied upon it, as we shall understand later in the discussion of formulaic phrases characteristic of oral epic.

The question of whether Homer wrote down his poems or whether he dictated them is insoluble and, indeed, incidental to our study. It is more important to observe that at the end of a long tradition of oral versification came the *Iliad,* the work of a renowned singer. The Greeks said that his name was Homer, and with their judgment we should perhaps be satisfied.[10]

TOLSTOY'S INTEREST IN EPIC

Commentators on *War and Peace* who emphasize what seem to them the epic qualities of Tolstoy find support in the authority of the author, who regarded his masterpiece as "Homeric." Georg Lukacs, the Hungarian Marxist critic, discovers, "Tolstoy himself was well aware that his great novels were genuine epics. But it was not only himself who compared *War and Peace* with Homer— many known and unknown readers of the book had the same feeling." Lukacs adds that comparison with Homeric epic is the result of the "general trend" of the style of the novel rather than "an actual characteristic of the style itself."[11] Turgenev writes, "The spirit of an epic fills this vast work" while he praises the author's originality.[12]

In the course of critical discussions certain new things have been said but, at the same time, certain old things need to be said again. The truth seems to be that the term "epic" has been used so indiscriminately that as a critical instrument the word has become blunted.

While we concede that epics are unique and in many ways incomparable, we must remind ourselves that a major goal of comparison is contrast. Hence epics deriving from different traditions, when compared, may help define each other's uniqueness. T. S. Eliot in his essay "Tradition and the Individual Talent" expresses the kinship:

> We dwell with satisfaction upon the poet's difference from his predecessors, especially the immediate predecessors; we endeavor to find something that can be isolated in order to be enjoyed. Whereas if we approach a poet without this prejudice we shall often find that not only the best, but the most individual parts of his work may be those in which the dead poets, his ancestors, assert their immortality most vigorously.

This study approaches Homer's epics and Tolstoy's *War and Peace* through the analogy of genre—in this instance, the epic. The purpose of criticism by genre, as Northrop Frye in his *Anatomy of Criticism* reminds us, "is not so much to classify as to clarify traditions and affinities, thereby bringing out a large number of literary relationships that would not be noticed as long as there were no context established for them."[13] In view of affinities with other novels, *War and Peace* is a work of such vast proportions that it is not surprising to find the word "epic" associated with it, in spite of the author's anxiety that the work might not fit into any genre.

There is evidence that Tolstoy was deeply concerned about the genre of his masterpiece. Explaining his reasons for many false starts on the "story of 1812," the author indicated that he was hampered by tradition in both form and content. "I was afraid that my writing would fall into no existing genre, neither novel, nor tale, nor long poem, nor history (*ni romana, ni povesti, ni poemy, ni istorii*).[14] Reluctant to call his work a novel, he wrote to Katkov, editor of the journal in which the first installments were being published, and (underscoring the words for emphasis) asked him *"not to call the work a novel."*[15]

The author's interest in the genre of his work never ceased. In his diary of 1865 he left a note about the poetry of the novelist being found "in a picture of manners and customs based on an historical event: *The Odyssey, The Iliad*, 1805."[16] *Eighteen Hundred and Five*, significantly, is the first part of *War and Peace*, published in two sections, in February and March 1865, in the periodical *The Russian Messenger*. Mention of his own work with the epics of Homer suggests that Tolstoy regards his work as epic.

Three years later, in an article in the *Russian Archives*, Tolstoy affirmed that *War and Peace* is "not a novel, even less is it a poem, and still less an historical chronicle. *War and Peace* is what the author wished and was able to express in the form in which it is expressed."[17] Is Tolstoy writing a prose epic, or has he created a new form, unlike any traditional genre?

Tolsoy felt that every great artist is bound to create his

own form. Nevertheless, he acknowledged his indebtedness to the Homeric epic when many years later, referring to *War and Peace,* he told Gorky, "without false modesty, it is like the *Iliad.*"[18] Thus Tolstoy, like Plato centuries earlier, pays tribute to an ancient archetype, for if, as Plato insists, Homer is the teacher of other poets, we must look to Homer for the beginning of epic tradition. The influence of Homer on subsequent ages may be attributed to the fact that his epics mark the beginning of what we may call civilization—not the temporal beginning but the ἀρχή (*arche*), the unique source to which we constantly revert in order to reorient ourselves as we reach each new stage of development.

Repeatedly Tolstoy has acknowledged indebtedness to the Homeric archetype, with which he became acquainted early in his literary career. His earliest writing mentions Homer. In *Sevastopol in May* (1855), a sketch based upon the author's experience in the Crimean campaign, Tolstoy praises men like Homer's heroes who seek glory in the midst of incredible suffering.

In his list of the writings which had the greatest effect on him from twenty to thirty-five years of age, he notes, under titles, "the *Iliad,*" and under degree of influence, "very great."[19] Tolstoy's biographers find significant his discovery of Homer. Statements by leading biographers observe that Tolstoy read the *Iliad,* in translation, for the first time in 1857, when he was twenty-nine years old. Aylmer Maude,[20] the English biographer who knew Tolstoy intimately, indicates in his *The Life of Tolstoy: First Fifty Years* that when in 1857 Tolstoy first read the *Iliad* he was greatly impressed.[21] Ernest J. Simmons, in his *Leo Tolstoy,* asserts that Tolstoy, returning to his estate, Yasnaya Polyana, after the grand tour of Europe in 1857, was brooding over literary projects and at that time read the "wonderful *Iliad*."[22] The Russian biographer, Paul Birukoff, confirms that in August 1857 Tolstoy studied the "remarkable" *Iliad*.[23] The author's diary of August 24 reads, "Read Homer—delightful! . . . Read the enchanting *Iliad*. Hephaistos and his works." (Here Tolstoy refers to the shield of Achilles, fashioned by the blacksmith god and depicting the civilization of the age.) The diary of August 29 (the day after the author's thirtieth birthday anniversary) reads, "Finished reading the incredibly delightful conclusion of the *Iliad!*"[24]

Tolsoy again read the *Iliad* in translation between 1860 and 1862,[25] the year before he began writing *War and Peace*. So much impressed by the merit of the epic was he that he began teaching the *Iliad* to pupils in the school for peasant children which he had opened on his estate. Emancipating the peasants, by government act of 1861, seemed to Tolstoy ineffectual. He felt it necessary to teach them reading, writing, and the rules of arithmetic to equip them for the use of freedom.

Pursuing a unique pedagogy, Tolstoy attempted to lead his pupils from the simple language of folklore—myths, legends, Russian proverbs—to more difficult types of literature by resorting to, among other writings, the *Iliad*. (His method is familiar today to educators aware that the teaching of literature must recapitulate its history.) The teacher did not anticipate difficulties for, as his early tracts on education tell us, the *Iliad* and the *Bible*, since they spring from the people itself, are intelligible to all men everywhere. Much later, in *What Is Art?* the author gives examples of literature comprehensible to all men in all times: the *Iliad*, the *Odyssey*, stories of Hebrew patriarchs and prophets, the psalms, parables from the gospels, and the hymns of the Vedas.[26]

Initiating his pupils to his original pedagogy, Tolstoy attempted to read Gynedich's translation of the *Iliad*, filled with pompous archaisms. The pupils were greatly perplexed; they thought the epic was written in French. Tolsoy related the plot, but the story made little impression on their minds. Eventually one of the more logical pupils was struck by the image of Phoebus Apollo, with clanking arrows at his back, flying down from Mount Olympus, and he asked, "But why did he not smash to pieces as he flew down from the mountain?" Tolstoy answered, "According to their idea he was a god." "A god?" asked the pupil. "But were there not many of them? Then he was not the real God."[27] Here Tolstoy shows the rift between the world of peasant children and that of the educated gentry.

Tolsoy's precepts at this time, and later, are aptly summarized by Isaiah Berlin: "That God exists, or that the *Iliad* is beautiful, or that men have a right to be free and also to be equal, are all eternal and absolute truths."[28] By September of 1862, however, Tolstoy's zeal for teaching truths to peasant children was beginning to wane and the author was eager to return to literary work. An entry in the diary of 1862 expresses a desire to write something truly magnificent. "The epic type would be a natural one for me," he remarked.[29] Then followed more than five years of creative activity. The result was *War and Peace*, written between 1863 and 1869.

After exhausting labor on *War and Peace*, with time on his hands, Tolstoy confided to his friend Fet, a prominent lyrical poet living as a country gentleman on a nearby estate, that the hours seemed dead. For a time he read and wrote nothing. In the winter of 1870 Fet was bewildered to learn that Tolstoy was studying Greek. Knowledge of Greek would enable him to read the New Testament in the original as well as classical authors. From the winter of 1870 until the early months of 1871 Tolstoy spent his waking hours studying ancient Greek. Simmons comments, "Like an arrogant schoolboy, he boasted to friends that he read Plato and Homer in the original and to Fet he wrote that he was living in Athens and at night spoke Greek in his sleep."[30] Fet, who felt sure that Tolstoy would not succeed in mastering the language, offered his own skin as parchment for a diploma when his friend was qualified to receive it. At length Tolstoy was able to boast in a letter to Fet, "I am writing nothing, only learning," and he continued, "your skin (to be used as parchment for my diploma in Greek) is in some danger. Improbable and astounding as it may seem, I have read Xenophon, and can now read him at sight. For Homer, a dictionary and some effort is still necessary."[31]

The simplicity of the Greek language, the clarity "like water fresh from the spring," appealed to Tolstoy, in contrast to the verbosity of translations based upon German texts. Tolstoy came to the conclusion that "without a knowledge of Greek there is no education."[32]

In the years that followed he passed on that knowledge to his children, in whose education he took a keen interest. When the children were old enough, he taught them Greek. First he taught the alphabet and then he started them reading Xenophon without benefit of knowledge of grammar.

Perhaps his interest in Greek yielded an extraneous reward. Simmons suggests that appointment for a Greek lesson may have saved Tolstoy from a less serious venture. He relates that despite the effort to resist the attraction of a handsome servant girl in the house, Tolstoy one day made an assignation. On his way to the encounter, his young son called from the window to remind him of the promised Greek lesson—thus interrupting the rendezvous. An autobiographical incident in "The Devil," a short story written in 1889 and published posthumously, parallels the author's experience.[33]

It is noteworthy that Tolstoy's proficiency in ancient Greek was gained not without a price. Enervated by labor on *War and Peace* he became seriously ill. His wife, worried that her husband's intense application to the study of Greek might further affect his health, urged him to go to the steppes for a koumys cure (of soured and fermented mare's milk). Yielding to his wife's persuasion, he set out with his brother-in-law to Samara, where he lived with the nomads in a tent on the open steppes and drank koumys. With him he took his Greek lexicon. To Fet he wrote, "I'm reading Herodotus, who describes in detail and with great accuracy these same galakto-fagatious [gluttonous-for-milk] Scythians among whom I am living."[34] For a time he read Greek with an ancient teacher among the visitors to Samara. Before the six-week sojourn had ended, however, his interest waned, and the huge Greek dictionary he had taken with him was used by his brother-in-law to press a collection of native wild flowers.

With regard to the cause of Tolstoy's malady, biographers differ. Simmons regards the author's absorption in the study of Greek as a symptom rather than the cause of his physical and spiritual ill health.[35] Simmons reminds us that the spiritual crisis of Tolstoy's later life had its roots in the period of the sixties. Though at this time the author was supremely happy in his married life, and though his wife had borne him four children during the writing of *War and Peace*, he was deeply troubled spiritually. He felt that there was a higher good than family happiness.

Nor did the praise of critics solace him. The distinguished critic N. N. Strakhov, who became one of Tolstoy's admired friends, had described *War and Peace* as "A complete picture of human life. A complete picture of the Russia of that day." Indifferent to literary fame, Tolstoy, reading the judgment, calmly remarked to his wife, "N. N. Strakhov has placed *War and Peace* on the pinnacle where it will remain in the opinion of society."[36] With the publication of *War and Peace* the author's reputation was assured. Nevertheless, Simmons concludes, "In a nature divided against itself, material success simply intensified the struggle between good and evil."[37]

Unlike Simmons, Maude attributes the author's ill health to a more specific conflict, the inability to reconcile two disparate points of view. Maude writes, "Tolstoy felt the charm of the literary art of the ancient world, and so keen was his power of entering into the minds of those of whom he read, and so different to his own was the Greek outlook upon life, that the contradiction produced in him a feeling of melancholy and apathy profound enough to affect his health." Maude concludes, "What clash of ideals it was that produced this result we may guess when we consider how from his earliest years Tolstoy had been attracted by the Christian ideals of meekness, humility, and self-sacrifice, and how little this accords with the outlook on life of the ancient Greeks."[38] That clash of ideals had not been resolved when Tolstoy wrote *What Is Art?* published in 1898, after fifteen years of reflection.

In *What Is Art?* Tolstoy's thoughts return to the ancient Greeks, whose works he uses as illustrations of religious perception, a quality essential to the best art. He draws examples from Greek and Hebrew cultures. "Thus, for instance, among the Greeks art transmitting the feeling of beauty, strength, and courage (Hesiod, Homer, Phidias) was chosen. . . ." Among the Jews "art transmitting feelings of devotion, and submission to the God of the Hebrews (the epic of Genesis, the prophets, the Psalms) was chosen. . . ."[39]

As an exponent of Christian culture, however, Tolstoy feels impelled to castigate the Greeks, although his disciple Maude comes to his aid. Defending Tolstoy the critic, Maude cautions: "He says what he means, and if anything he rather overstates it. . . . If, for instance, when insisting that man's moral ideals advance, he says that it is not the very best that can be done by the art of nations after 1900 years of Christian teaching, to choose as the ideal of this life the ideal that was held by a small, semi-savage, slave-holding people who lived 2000 years ago, we should not overlook the fact that he quite realizes that those old Greeks really did, as he says, 'imitate the nude human body extremely well,' and did 'erect buildings pleasant to look at. . . .' "[40]

We are reminded of a clash of ideals that occurred much earlier, between Aristotle and Plato, arguing the ethics of Homeric epic. Aristotle tells us that epic is the source of other genres, such as tragedy, and that when tragedy fell heir to epic poetry the graver spirits imitated noble

21

actions and the actions of good men (*Poetics*, 1448 b
25–26). Aristotle concludes that, like epic, tragedy pre-
serves the type and yet ennobles it. In this manner
Achilles is portrayed by Homer (*Poetics*, 1454 b 14–15).
Even when killing Hector, Achilles is portrayed in Homer
by the conventional epithet δῖos, noble or godlike (XXII,
364).

While the gods of Homer are hardly models of
rectitude, a man could receive no higher praise than to be
likened to a god. Plato, however, sensitive to the moral
influence of Homer, since Homer's epics were valued not
only for delight but also for instruction, would advise
expurgating Homer. Plato would teach that the gods can
do no wrong. Although Plato acknowledges that from
earliest youth he had always had an "awe and love of
Homer," he warns that a man is not to be reverenced
more than the truth (*Republic*, 595).

We understand more clearly Plato's derogation of
Homer when we realize that Plato's entire philosophy is
built upon the conception of the Idea of Good, ἀγαθόν, a
universal pattern descending from the model of heroic
arete. The adjective ἀγαθός, which corresponds to the
noun *arete*, though it derives from a different root, sometimes meant "noble" and sometimes "brave," but in
Homer's time it seldom meant "good" any more than *arete*
meant moral virtue.[41] The Greek philosophic tradition,
however, imbued later with the ideal of *arete* in the
Platonic sense, was largely absorbed by the Christian
tradition and flourished again among the humanists of the
Renaissance. In time, from the primitive conception of
arete, the ideal of man's perfection, we see a gradual
development of a universal pattern applicable to men

everywhere. Thus Homer the educator of Greece, because he sees life as governed by universal laws, becomes in time the teacher of humanity.

WAR AND PEACE *AS EPIC*

Before Tolstoy began writing *War and Peace* he had become well known for his vivid depiction of military experience in the Caucasus and at the siege of Sevastopol—sketches based upon observation during service in the army, first in the sporadic wars against the Caucasian mountain tribes and later in the Crimean War.

When Tolstoy went to the Caucasus in 1851 he had no intention of entering the army; hence he had left his identification papers and other official documents behind. Lack of these documents, which he was unable to obtain, delayed his promotion and subsequent receipt of a commission and prevented his receiving a St. George's Cross, for which he had been recommended.

His story *The Raid* is based upon experiences in the summer of 1851 when, before entering the service, he had taken part as a volunteer in an expedition against the Caucasian mountain tribes. In 1852 his first published novel, *Childhood,* appeared in the leading Petersburg monthly, *The Contemporary,* and was received enthusiastically by both critics and readers. He was now a Cadet.

In 1853 he began writing *The Cossacks,* which he submitted unfinished to the publisher, M. N. Katkov. The story was published in 1863.

In 1854 he received his commission "for distinguished conduct in action against the mountaineers." In February 1854, returning from a leave of absence, Tolstoy traveled

2,000 miles by horse to meet forces in service in Turkey and subsequently joined the siege of Sevastopol. After action involving "serious danger," he was placed in charge of a mountain platoon, where he remained until the end of the siege. He had been removed from Sevastopol on instruction of Alexander II, who, pleased with the author's sketch *Sevastopol in December*, ordered, "Take care of the life of that young man."

On his last visit to Sevastopol Tolstoy wrote to his aunt, September 4, 1855, "On the 27th there was a great and glorious fight at Sevastopol. I had the fortune and misfortune to reach the town on the very day of the assault, so that I was able to witness it and even take some part in the action as a volunteer." The following day, "my birthday," as he records it, was a "sad and memorable day," the day of the fall of Sevastopol. He added, "During these last days the thought of definitely leaving the army has occurred to me more and more often and insistently."

In March 1856 he became a Lieutenant. He was now in Petersburg. After applying for a discharge, he was allowed at length to resign his commission. Unimpeded except by the Censor who had plagued him during his early career as author-artilleryman, he now had time to reflect upon future endeavors. In his diary of September 18, 1855, the day before tendering his resignation from the army, Tolstoy wrote, "My aim is literary fame and the good I can accomplish by my writings."[42]

Among the "trials of the pen" the author already had to his credit twenty stories, many of an autobiographical nature, such as his recollections of military exploits in *The Raid*, and the three Sevastopol sketches, *The Cossacks*, as well as the partially autobiographical accounts of domestic

24

life, such as *Childhood, Boyhood,* and *Youth.* As can be observed, Tolstoy's life had already become a rich source of information for his work.

The twenty stories written at the beginning of his career were published in the first collected edition of 1864. By this time Tolstoy was deeply absorbed in the writing of *War and Peace.* He had already discarded introductory chapters of two novels, one concerning the Decembrist Revolt of 1825 and the other describing the return of a Decembrist hero in 1856, after many years of confinement in a Siberian prison.[43] In the course of his deliberation about the hero's misfortunes, the author became convinced that to understand his character's actions he must study the period dealing with the hero's youth. Such investigation led him to lay aside all he had written and to plunge into the notable year 1812. In the second draft he explained why he had to move back to the period of the Decembrist's youth, which coincided with the period of 1812, "so glorious for Russian," for as he explained, "The odors and sounds of that time are still dear to us but also so remote from us that now we can think about them calmly."[44]

Like Homer, Tolstoy returns to an earlier age, *in illo tempore,* to gain historic perspective. Looking backward, Homer brings the past into the panoramic view of the future when he foretells "the day shall come for holy Ilios to be laid low" and Tolstoy, having walked over the battlefield at Borodino, describes events which occurred a half century earlier, when in 1812 the "holy" city, Moscow (*Moscou la sainte,* in the words of Napoleon), was laid low—both cities destroyed by fire.

As Tolstoy's original hero receded further into the

background, other figures, partly historical and partly fictional, began to enter his work. To understand the action of the new characters the author's imagination carried him back still further to the year 1805, at which time he made the final beginning. He explained the reason thus: "For the third time I turned back to an earlier period, guided by a feeling that may seem strange to the majority of readers but which, I hope, will be understood by those whose opinions I value. I did it guided by a feeling similar to shyness that I cannot define in a single word. I was ashamed to write about our triumph in the struggle against Bonaparte's France without having described our failures and our shame."[45] The final design included a trilogy of which *War and Peace* was to be the first book. Events of 1825 and 1856 were to be described later. Though the last two books were never written, the author never abandoned the desire to write about the Decembrists.

When at length Tolstoy began writing *War and Peace* he had not yet conceived of the course of events or the characters he was later to depict in his vast epic. Against an historical background, he intended to describe the family life of the Russian aristocracy. There was no indication of the forthcoming emphasis on war and no trace of the author's elaborate philosophy of history.

The first part of the book, the story of family life among the nobility in the year 1805, was published under the title *Eighteen Hundred and Five*.[46] During the autumn and winter of 1865 the design of the work expanded and by the end of the year the third part was ready for the printer. Convinced that he was now engaged in a major undertaking, the author yielded to the persuasion of his wife to publish the work in book form rather than serially. The sixth and last volume of *War and Peace* appeared in 1869.

As in the depiction of a number of characters in his earlier writings, Tolstoy again resorted to life as a source of information for his art. Many of the author's kinfolk are commonly regarded as prototypes of the fictional characters. From letters, diaries, anecdotes, and especially from the records of his grandparents, the Tolstoys and the Volkonskys, the author found suggestions for modeling his heroes and heroines. In general, members of Tolstoy's father's family are represented by the Rostovs and members of his mother's family by the Bolkonskys. Thus old Count Ilya Tolstoy, the author's paternal grandfather, becomes the prototype of old Count Rostov, and old Prince Nicholas Sergeyevich Volkonsky, the author's maternal grandfather, becomes the prototype of old Prince Nicholas Ilych Bolkonsky. And, in further parallels, the son of Count Rostov, Nicholas, and the daughter of Prince Bolkonsky, Mary, in the fictional marriage in the epilogue repeat the event in life, the union of the author's parents.

Although Tolstoy's mother died before he was two years old and his father before he was eight, the author recalls some of the admirable characteristics he discovered about his parents, and these traits he recorded in *War and Peace*. Like Tolstoy's father, the fictional young Nicholas Rostov participates in the campaign of 1812 against Napoleon, and after his marriage to Princess Mary Bolkonskaya settles on the estate Bald Hills—the Yasnaya Polyana of Tolstoy's father—and manages his affairs well. Like Tolstoy's mother, the fictional Princess Mary, notable for her modesty, is well educated by a stern father, a former general under Catherine II. Tolstoy's mother, as an only child, received at her father's hands the discipline the old Prince might otherwise have reserved for a son.

Significant it is, however, that Tolstoy gives Prince Bolkonsky a son, Prince Andrew, and significant too is the author's reason. In a letter addressed to L. I. Volkonskaya, who had asked who was represented by the character named Andrew Bolkonsky, Tolstoy replied:

In the Battle of Austerlitz, which will be described later, but with which I began the novel, I needed a brilliant young man to be killed. Later in the novel, I needed only the old Bolkonsky and his daughter. But since it is awkward to describe a character not connected with anything in the novel, I have decided to make the brilliant young man a son of the old Bolkonsky. Then he caught my interest, a role appeared for him later in the novel, and I took mercy on him, only wounding him severely instead of killing him. [47]

In the early sections of the book, describing events culminating in the defeat of forces opposing Napoleon at the battle of Austerlitz in 1805, the influence of Homeric epic seems most apparent. Remarkable, too, is the fact that the salient example of Homeric heroism is the fictional character Prince Andrew, who, as a figment of the author's imagination, is commonly regarded as a counterpart of the author himself. In that role he stands as a transitional figure revealing Tolstoy's development in the conception of heroism, exemplifying first Homeric, then Christian ideals. Although the early Prince Andrew has a number of Homeric attributes, he dies a Christian hero.

Perhaps Tolstoy's family and friends, to whom he read the initial part of the book and who delighted in seeing themselves portrayed as characters, identified no member of the group with Prince Andrew because of an inconsistency resulting from the author's own dilemma—the difficulty of transforming a Homeric archetypal hero into a Christian antitype. Tolstoy's wife, who copied the manuscript many times, expressed a favorable opinion of Andrew's sister. "I like everything about Princess Mary!" she said. But of the brother of the Princess she remarked that the characterization was "not yet entirely clear."[48]

As the author has indicated, Prince Andrew of the early work, *Eighteen Hundred and Five*, was destined to be killed in battle, but his life was spared by the author. Prince Andrew, like Achilles, was first designed as a short-lived hero who would die gloriously, "leaving manhood and youth," according to the Homeric lament. Before comparing the heroic ideals represented by Achilles and Prince Andrew, let us look briefly at the development of the ideal of heroism underlying epic tradition. Thereafter we may observe more clearly the development of Prince Andrew, first as a Homeric hero similar to the archetypal Achilles, then as a Christian hero, an antitype.

Chapter II

GREEK ARCHETYPE
TO CHRISTIAN ANTITYPE

FROM ACHILLES to Christ, from the classical archetype of the *Iliad* to the Christian antitype of the
Gospels, Prince Andrew undergoes transformation.

In tracing the development of the Homeric archetype,
comments by Werner Jaeger in *Paideia* are helpful.[1]
Jaeger emphasizes a concept basic to all epics, that of the
heroic ideal, which is manifest in the expanding implications of the word *arete* (excellence). The Greek word *arete*
implies the creation of a definite ideal of human perfection, a standard by which to measure a man's achievement
as he reaches each new stage of development.

We trace a clue to the history of this heroic ideal in the
changing implications of the word *arete*. *Arete* is initially
the attribute of a nobleman. The root of the word is the
same as that of *aristos*, the superlative of the adjective
meaning *good*. In the plural the word denotes the nobility.

In a warlike age of great migrations, such as Homer's, it
was natural that a man should be valued primarily for his
prowess in battle. Homer generally uses the word *arete* to
denote the hero's strength, and above all his heroic valor,
although valor is not considered a heroic quality distinct
from strength.

Achilles' superhuman strength is revealed repeatedly. A
salient example occurs in the episode in which Patroclus
dons the armor of Achilles before going into battle. Patroclus

31

receives from Achilles all weapons but the Pelian spear which the centaur Chiron had given Achilles' father. That spear Achilles alone has strength to wield (XVI, 140–144). Again Achilles' superior strength is demonstrated in the last book of the *Iliad*. Achilles has fastened the door of his hut with a bolt which can be moved only by the strength of three men or by the power of a god, in this instance Hermes (XXIV, 453–457).

Homer indicates also that surpassing strength and prowess are the basis of leadership. Hence it is impossible to dissociate leadership and *arete*. In his role as leader Achilles excels both as "speaker of words and as doer of deeds," preeminent in both oratory and battle. The dual role of Achilles is represented in the scene of the Embassy to Achilles in the ninth book of the *Iliad*. Although here we find three envoys, Ajax, Odysseus, and Achilles' old tutor Phoenix, in the earlier version, according to Jaeger, there were only two envoys, Ajax embodying the element of action and Odysseus the element of speech—the two disparate aspects which Achilles unites, thus fulfulling the highest powers of body and mind.[2]

As the Greeks themselves, following the vision of Homer, acquired in the course of history a clearer perception of their aim in life, the old aristocratic view of Homer became increasingly intellectualized until it attained paramount significance in the fifth and fourth centuries B.C. In the fifth century the goal of molding a man as he ought to be was not new to the "sculptor of men," Sophocles, nor was the ideal of the beautiful and the good, *kalos kagathos,* unfamiliar to the philosophers of the fourth century. The magnanimous man of Aristotle's *Nicomachean Ethics* is witness enough.

Aristotle explains that the desire for complete *arete* is the result of an ennobled self-love, φιλαυτία.[3] This ideal, deeply rooted in the old aristocratic code of morality, is comprehensible when we realize that the self of which Aristotle speaks is not the physical self but the ideal which inspires one, the ideal which every nobleman seeks to realize in his lifetime. The highest kind of self-love inspires a man to "take possession of the beautiful,"[4] to sacrifice himself for his friends or his country in order to "take possession of the beautiful."[5] The strange phrase, difficult to translate, is repeated. We grasp something of its import when we realize that beauty meant nobility also, and he who was noble lost no opportunity of winning the prize of the highest *arete*. "For," says Aristotle, "such a man would prefer short intense pleasures to long quiet ones; would choose to live nobly for a year rather than to pass many years of ordinary life; would rather do one great and noble deed than many small ones." It is clear that many aspects of Aristotle's ideal self-love are derived from Homer's representation of Achilles, for we note that Achilles, in conformity to the ethics of his age, is "noble," even while he is slaying Hector. Homer tells us, "Then to the dead man spake noble Achilles," as he drew forth his spear from the body of the slain Hector (XXII, 364). Homeric epic and Athenian philosophy are bound together by the continuing vitality of the old Homeric ideal of *arete*.

The fact that culture as reflected in the Homeric epic was originally restricted to a special class, the aristocracy, did not prevent later generations from insisting that more men should share its benefits. Thus the democratic culture of Periclean Athens reached its zenith as the result of the gradual extension of the early aristocratic tradition. Unlike Homer's aristocrats, however, later generations did not think in terms of a privileged class of landed nobility, but in terms of *arete*, and thus attributed to nobility a universal meaning. Though Homer's epics and Greek philosophy have in common the exploration of the position of man in the universe, the epic presents the problem in mythical terms, philosophy in rational terms.

Rationalizing the concept of *arete* gave scope for the transmission of that ideal. The aristocratic connotation of *arete* as it was later expanded to comprehend the ideal of *kalos kagathos* (the beautiful and the good) is comparable in Elizabethan England to that of the gentleman, a man who displays both in war and in courtly life standards which are not valid for the common man.[6] When we think of Hamlet, Prince of Denmark, "the courtier's, soldier's, scholar's, eye, tongue, sword," we recall that Achilles more than two millenia earlier was, like Hamlet, both "a speaker of words and a doer of deeds."

Nevertheless, to acknowledge the timeless significance of classical ideals revitalized in the Renaissance does not mean that we have given the Greeks authority over us which is absolute. The concomitant influence of the Christian tradition is evidence to the contrary. During the Middle Ages the concept of the value of the individual had become identified with a belief which Christianity did most to foster, that each soul is of infinite value in the eyes of God. Subsequently that Christian ideal acquired infinite possibilities. It embodied the purpose of later generations and justified the cultural expansion of both individual and state. Indeed, it transcended national boundaries to become a universal principle. The purpose of this study, however, is not to trace the widening implications of the word *arete*, but to relate that concept to the epic of Tolstoy, for the ideal of *arete* is palpable in modified form in *War and Peace*.

The heroic ideal, revealed in *War and Peace* first as the privilege of a chosen few, is later extended to include a whole people. It permeates the lives of the Russian populace, making them give to their country the glory they might have kept for themselves. It extends beyond the limits of patriotism, such as is implicit in the allegiance of Homer's Hector, who fights not only for personal glory but also for his native land. In Tolstoy's epic the ideal of heroism attached first to the individual such as Prince Andrew, then to the nation represented by its chosen leader General Kutuzov, embraces in its third and final form the vision of primitive Christianity. That vision is expressed most significantly by the "Christian" peasant, Platon Karataev, the embodiment of the Christian ethic which regards aspirations to personal glory as vanity. Ultimately, in attaching the implications of *arete* to the values of Christendom, Tolstoy has created an ideal of heroism antithetical to Homeric tradition. Instead of a Homeric archetype we now have a Tolstoyan antitype.

Let us return to the Homeric significance of the concept of *arete*, which lies at the heart of all great epics. Homeric epic reveals that victory in battle is the final test of heroism. Such victory is proof not only of physical prowess but also of superior *arete*. A necessary concomitant of *arete* is honor, *kudos*, conferred upon the hero as reward of his merit, his *arete*. The denial of honor due is the greatest of human errors, for Homer's heroes measure their own worth, their *arete*, by the opinion which others hold of them. To honor a man for his *arete* is a primitive instinct on the basis of which we can understand the tragic conflict of Achilles, in whom the quintessence of the Homeric ideal of heroism is embodied. Achilles' wrath resulting in his refusal to aid his allies does not spring from exaggerated ambition. A great ambition is for the early Greek a quality of a great hero. When Agamemnon infringes upon Achilles' honor by robbing him of his prize of war, Briseis, Agamemnon loses sight of true *arete*, the *arete* of the noble Achilles. Achilles has suffered insult at the hands of Agamemnon; a preeminent *arete* has been denied its honor. Accordingly, Achilles' mother, Thetis, entreats Zeus, "Honor my son, who must die sooner than all others. Agamemnon has robbed him of his honor; do you honor him, Olympian!" (I, 506–508).[7] Thereupon Zeus is gracious to Achilles in fulfilling his mother's entreaty.

Like Achilles, every Homeric hero claims the honor due him, for recognition of his honor, his *kudos*, is implicit in the concept of *arete*. It is expressed in the motto of heroism throughout the centuries:

αἰὲν ἀριστεύειν καὶ ὑπείροχον ἔμμεναι ἄλλων.

Ever to be the best and to excel all others (VI, 208).

The motto is uttered by the Trojan Glaucus who, when he meets the Achaean Diomedes on the battlefield, wishes to prove himself a worthy opponent:

Hippolochus begat me, and I claim to be his son. He sent me to Troy, and often gave me this command, to strive always for the highest arete, *and to excel all others. (VI, 206–208)*[8]

The motto is repeated in the eleventh book of the *Iliad,* which represents Peleus giving the same counsel to his son Achilles (XI, 784).

Even in later times, when men obeyed an inner standard rather than the standard of Homeric society which measured a man's *arete* by the opinion others held of him, the initial import of *arete* was not forgotten. Aristotle describes honor as a standard for measuring man's attainment of *arete.* "Men seem to pursue honor in order to assure themselves of their own worth—their *arete.* They strive to be honored for it, by men who know them and are judicious."[8]

The Greeks believed that aspiration to individual honor was justified since it brought a man closer to his goal, the achievement of "immortal glory among mortals." Hector is cognizant of that goal when, about to die at Achilles' hands, he implores Achilles, "At least let me not die without a struggle or ingloriously, but in some great deed of arms whereof men yet to be born shall hear" (XXII, 304–305). The hero's glory is his immortality and it is a heroic paradox that by dying gloriously the hero may achieve immortal life. Accordingly, Homer rewards his epic heroes with nothing but pagan immortality, the memory in the minds of men of the hero's glorious deeds. Homeric epic thus becomes an expression of early Greek escatology.

Thus far we have analyzed the concept of *arete* as it leads to the goal of *kudos,* personal glory. Another concept implicit in the idea of *arete* is that of *aidos,* a sense of duty which enjoins a man to honor the heroic traditions of his ancestors. Expressed negatively, *aidos* constrains a man not to dishonor (put to shame) his illustrious ancestors.

According to the heroic code of both Homer and Tolstoy the elders serve as examples for young men to follow—let youth not bring dishonor upon their noble progenitors. Every nobleman educates his son by presenting to him an eternal ideal; it is the son's duty to conform. Hence Glaucus, having traced his illustrious lineage, recalls his father's final injunction concerning *aidos*, not to "put to shame" the race of his fathers that were of noble blood (VI, 209). Hector, likewise, utters the code emphatically when he denies his wife's entreaty to refrain from battle:

> *I have very sore shame* (aidos) *of the Trojans and Trojan dames with trailing robes, if like a coward I shrink away from battle. Moreover mine own soul forbiddeth me, seeing I have learnt ever to be valiant and fight in the forefront of the Trojans, winning my father's great glory and mine own. (VI, 441–447)*

Hector's prayer for his son, before the final parting, expresses ardently the hereditary concepts of both *kudos* and *aidos*:

> *O Zeus and all ye gods, vouchsafe ye that this my son may likewise prove even as I, preeminent amid the Trojans, and as valiant in might, and be a great king of Ilios. Then may men say of him, "Far greater is he than his father" as he returneth home from battle; and may he bring with him bloodstained spoils from the foeman he hath slain, and may his mother's heart be glad. (VI, 476–481)*

PRINCE ANDREW

Was Tolstoy thinking of Homer's code of honor, with its dual obligations of *kudos* and *aidos*, when he placed in the mouth of old Prince Bolkonsky words reminiscent of

Hector's prayer for his son? The old prince reminds his son Andrew, who is about to depart for battle:

> *Remember this, Prince Andrew, if they kill you it will hurt me, your old father . . . but if I hear that you have not behaved like a son of Nicholas Bolkonsky, I shall be ashamed! (114)*

Prince Andrew's answer to his father reveals that the exhortation was unnecessary. Anticipating the birth of a child, Prince Andrew pleads:

> *If I'm killed, and if I have a son, do not let him be taken away from you . . . let him grow up with you. . . . Please. (114)*

Thus the code of honor will be perpetuated.

Tolstoy gives Prince Andrew a son who, like Hector's son, is soon to become an orphan. We recall the foreboding of Hector's wife, Andromache, as she reflects upon the dire future of her son, Astyanax, as she prophesies the ignominious treatment of an orphan (XXII, 487–507). Andrew's son, a lonely orphan boy of fifteen at the close of the book, is dreaming of his father. In his dream he envisions himself marching at the head of an immense army and in front of him floats glory. He is wearing a helmet such as he has seen in illustrations from his Plutarch. As he comes nearer the goal the phantom form of his father appears before him and he wakes. "My father!" little Nicholas thinks—for he never thought of his father in human form. "My father has been with me and caressed me. He approved of me. . . . Whatever he may tell me, I would do it. Mucius Scaevola burned his hand. Why should not the same thing happen to me? I know they want me to learn. And I will learn. But some day I shall have finished learning, and then I will do something." Little Nicholas prays that he may be far greater than Plutarch's men, as he pledges his father, "Father! Father! Yes, I will do something with which even he would be satisfied. . . ." (1309)

And now let me ask indulgence, once for all, for the tiresome summaries of plot which the nature of this study makes necessary. True to epic tradition, both Homer and Tolstoy create a short-lived hero who will win glory before his death. In Homer few, like Odysseus' dog, live out the normal span of life. Achilles is thrice reminded of his early death by his mother Thetis, who laments, "Now art thou made short-lived and lamentable beyond all men" (I, 416–417).[10] He is again reminded by his immortal horse Xanthus (XIX, 409) and by the dying Hector who warns of the "wrath of gods, in the day when Paris and Phoebus Apollo slay thee, for all thy valor, at the Skaian gate" (XXII, 358–360). Finally the phantom form of Patroclus prophesies, "Yea and thou too thyself, Achilles dear to gods, beneath the wall of the noble Trojans art doomed to die" (XXIII, 80–81).

The prophetic warnings go unheeded, for Achilles grieves not that he is to die early but that he may have too little time in which to display valor. He deliberately chooses the short, honorable path to glory rather than the long, ignoble passage to oblivion when he considers, "If I abide here and besiege the Trojans' city, then my returning home is taken from me, but my fame shall be imperishable; but if I go home to my dear native land, my high fame is taken from me, but my life shall endure long while, neither shall the issue of death soon reach me" (IX, 412–416).

Achilles anticipates his early death when he is about to slay the unarmed son of Priam, Lycaon, who as a suppliant clings with one hand to the knees of Achilles and with the other grasps Achilles' spear. Achilles reflects, "There cometh morn or eve or some noonday when my life too some man shall take in battle, whether with spear he smite or arrow from the string" (XXI, 111–113).

As in the example of Achilles, the death of the short-lived hero Prince Andrew is foretold after the battle of Austerlitz, but the rumor is false and Prince Andrew is saved to become a Christian hero. Like Achilles, Prince Andrew is a "brilliant young man to be killed," but the author allows him at the end of the Austrian campaign to be wounded merely, because "a role appeared for him later"—the role of a Christian hero.

Let us trace briefly the wrath theme in the *Iliad* and then compare it with the theme of the wrath and reconciliation of Prince Andrew. Notably the wrath of both heroes is engendered by an insult done to honor— whether honor in war or honor in love. The first word of the *Iliad*, "wrath," announces the theme and foretells the heroic action of Achilles. Though dishonored by Agamemnon, who later offers appeasement, Achilles while rejecting Agamemnon's offer yet remains at the siege of Troy in order that he may eventually fight, die, and leave an immortal name.

Homer reveals Achilles with the passion of an early age— wrath engendered by pride because his honor has been impugned. But Achilles' pride exceeds the exigencies of insulted honor. Even the gods can unbend, Achilles is warned, and theirs is "loftier majesty and honor and might" (IX, 497–498). Achilles is cautioned that he may "fall and pay the price" (IX, 512). That price he is willing to pay, as his refusal of Agamemnon's offer indicates. The prayer of his mother Thetis, that her son's countrymen suffer defeat until they miss him, is fulfilled, but at the expense of Patroclus' life. Now Achilles perceives the irony of the fulfillment. The death of Patroclus, who was dearer to Achilles than all Agamemnon's gifts, is Homer's "nemesis" for the pride of Achilles. Though Achilles' honor is restored by the humiliation of Agamemnon, Achilles has no joy in the outcome. "May strife perish utterly among gods and men, and wrath that stirreth even a wise man to be vexed," he cries (XVIII, 107–108). Nevertheless, he will get revenge upon the slayer of Patroclus, Hector, before he accepts his own death. The death of Hector closes the revenge motif; with the slaying of Hector, Achilles' wrath is appeased. Acceptance of ransom from King Priam, who has come as a suppliant to claim the body of his son Hector, marks the termination of the wrath theme.

Like Achilles, Prince Andrew is proud. Before he leaves to join Kutuzov in the Austrian campaign, he is reminded by his sister Mary, as she offers him an ikon, "You are good in every way, Andrew, but you have a kind of intellectual pride" (109). After a few words of banter, Prince Andrew accepts the blessing of the holy ikon with his sister's assurance, "Against your will He will save and will have mercy on you and bring you to Himself" (110).

This is the young Andrew of the first part of *War and Peace* who has expressed admiration for the military exploits of his hero Napoleon. Later, after Vienna has been occupied by the French and Brunn is about to fall, Prince Andrew has mixed feelings. He continues to admire the genius of his hero Napoleon, but at the same time, like Achilles, he is resolved to win personal glory in defence of his countrymen, who are allied with the Austrians against the French. On the eve of the battle of Austerlitz Andrew, dreaming of triumphs, expresses a Homeric desire. "Death, wounds, the loss of family—I fear nothing. And precious and dear as many persons are to me—father, sister, wife—yet dreadful and unnatural as it seems, I would give them all at once for a moment of glory . . ." (283–284).

After Prince Andrew has been wounded at the battle of Austerlitz his attitude toward war changes. Falling with the flagstaff in his hand, while attempting to hoist the flag over the cannons, Andrew, in an agony of pain, is aware for the first time of the lofty, infinite sky, the emblem of peace and triumph. As he lies on the field littered with dead and wounded, he is noticed by his hero Napoleon, who is making a tour of the battlefield. Napoleon stands over Andrew. "That's a fine death," says Napoleon, who was accustomed to take pleasure in observing the dead and wounded at the end of a battle.

Now Tolstoy speaks for Andrew: "He knew it was Napoleon—his hero—but at that moment Napoleon seemed to him such a small, insignificant creature in comparison with what was passing between himself and that lofty, infinite sky . . ." (312). As he is carried to the hospital tent Andrew remembers the ikon his sister has given him.

"It would be good," thought Prince Andrew, glancing at the ikon his sister had hung around his neck with such

emotion and reverence, "it would be good if everything were as clear and simple as it seems to Mary. How good it would be to know where to seek for help in this life, and what to expect after it beyond the grave! How happy and calm I should be if I could now say: 'Lord, have mercy on me!' . . . But to whom should I say that? Either to a Power indefinable, incomprehensible, which I not only cannot address but which I cannot even express in words—the Great All or Nothing" said he to himself, "or to that God who has been sewn into this amulet by Mary!" (314–315)

By his family Prince Andrew is supposed dead. "Your son," writes Kutuzov to the old Prince, "fell before my eyes, a standard in his hand and at the head of a regiment—he fell as a hero, worthy of his father and his fatherland" (346). Kutuzov expresses hope, since Andrew's name is not upon the list of officers found on the battlefield, that Prince Bolkonsky's son may yet be among the living. Kutuzov's hopes are not in vain. Tolstoy cannot let Prince Andrew die because, as the author has indicated, "a role appeared for him later."

The wounded Andrew returns home. On the night of his arrival a son is born, his wife dies. The death of Andrew's wife is significant because by freeing Andrew of family encumbrances the author has freed himself to develop the theme of love essential to the portrayal of a Christian hero. Let us trace the development of the new theme.

Recovering from wounds, Andrew is at first disillusioned. His quest for a meaning of life beyond his "atheistic convictions" (421) is revealed in his conversation with his friend Pierre Bezukhov, in the philosophic crossing on the ferry raft. The man of Christian convictions,

44

Pierre, acts as a foil—a Patroclus to Achilles. Tolstoy is here using an ancient device familiar to the creators of David and Jonathan, Don Quixote and Sancho, Hamlet and Horatio, to mention but a few characters paired in male friendship.

Tolstoy's representation of Andrew and Pierre, however, is more than a literary device. In the antithetical viewpoints expressed by the two characters, critics have discerned the author's own dubiety—an inner struggle perceptible in Tolstoy's youth and one which would result in a profound spiritual crisis. The debate between the dual embodiments of the author reaches its climax in the famous scene on the ferry.

Andrew, disappointed in his pursuit of glory and disturbed by a feeling of responsibility for his wife's death, finds no purpose in life. Pierre attempts to console him. "If there is a God and future life, there is truth and good, and man's highest happiness consists in striving to attain them. We must live, we must love, and we must believe that we live not only today on this scrap of earth, but have lived and shall live forever, there in the Whole," Pierre affirms, pointing to the sky (422).

Andrew, sensitive to the soft beauties of twilight, feels the sound of the waves whispering, "It is true, believe it." Aloud he answers Pierre, "Yes, if it only were so!" For the first time since he lay on the battlefield at Austerlitz, a feeling "joyful and youthful" awoke in Andrew's soul (422).

The meeting with Pierre is an "epoch" in Andrew's life, even though the feeling of exaltation does not continue unabated. A later meeting with Natasha Rostova lifts him from another period of despondency. As in the previous scene, the background of nature influences his mood. This time Tolstoy allows an old oak to speak.

The oak tree encountered in the forest in springtime reflects Prince Andrew's mood. To Andrew it seems that nature is yielding to the spell of spring, a feeling of rebirth is seizing the land—touching all except the old oak with its gnarled and sprawling branches. "Spring, love, happiness!" the old oak seems to say. "Are you not weary of that stupid, meaningless, constantly repeated fraud? Always the same and always a fraud! There is not spring, no sun, no happiness!" (459). Prince Andrew responds sympathetically. "Yes, the oak is right, a thousand times right," he reflects. "Let others—the young—yield afresh to that fraud, but we know life, our life is finished!" (459).

A short time later, on a business trip to the Rostov estate, Andrew glimpses Natasha, gay and laughing among her companions. "What is she so glad about? What is she thinking of?" Andrew asks himself. That night, unable to sleep, Andrew opens his window and hears Natasha, entranced by the moonlight, singing from the window above. "For her I might as well not exist!" he reflects. Then Tolstoy tells us, "In his soul there suddenly arose such an unexpected turmoil of youthful thoughts and hopes, contrary to the whole tenor of his life," that he is unable to explain his condition to himself (462). In this episode the author dramatizes the awakening of Andrew to new life. For Andrew, Natasha henceforth becomes the embodiment of human love, in a stage transitional to his acceptance of divine love. Love of a woman will lead to love of Christ.

Returning to his estate some time later, Andrew again encounters the symbolic oak, this time "quite transfigured, spreading out a canopy of sappy dark-green foliage." The "old scars" are nowhere evident on the century-old bark.

"Yes, it is the same oak," Prince Andrew concludes. Then Tolstoy tells us, "all at once he was seized by an unreasoning springtime feeling of joy and renewal" (462). With Prince Andrew's interest in Natasha the theme of love begins to replace the theme of military glory. The Homeric hero is gradually being transformed into a Christian hero.

For a brief interlude, however, Prince Andrew becomes absorbed in affairs of state. Having already observed the unheroic in military life in the person of his former hero Napoleon, he now seeks the "living ideal of the perfection toward which he strove" (471–472) in the exploits of the civil reformer Speranski. Eventually he is disappointed also in the efforts of the equally unheroic Speranski. Andrew, like Achilles, is "a speaker of words and a doer of deeds" until he perceives the futility of his endeavor. Finally unencumbered, he is ready to turn his attention to Natasha.

As the theme of love in its various manifestations develops, Andrew is temporarily revitalized. Dancing with Natasha at the ball he feels "revived and rejuvenated" (505). Subsequently he is moved to ask her hand in marriage, but the marriage, because of his father's objection, is postponed for a year.

Meanwhile, Natasha, impatient of waiting, attempts to elope with Anatole Kuragin. This episode, according to Tolstoy, in a letter addressed to P. I. Bartenev in 1867, is the "crux of the whole novel."[11] Certainly the episode is significant in the development of the character of Prince Andrew, for at this point the theme of wrath and revenge for insult done a proud man is initiated. We recall that the theme of wrath evolved in the *Iliad* when Agamemnon took from Achilles his beloved prize of war, Briseis, thus instigating Achilles' desire to avenge an insult done to honor and thus, as the result of Achilles' withdrawal from battle, leading to the climactic death of Patroclus. The revenge motif in tragic structure may be a very powerful one, as Frye observes. Essential to the action are the many female figures who "polarize the tragic conflict." In this list Frye includes Briseis.[12] He might have included Natasha.

Informed of Natasha's escapade, Andrew, deeply hurt, is able to forgive neither Natasha nor Anatole. Like Achilles, Andrew is adamant; he wants revenge. He rejoins the Army in order to encounter Anatole and to challenge him to a duel. At this stage he can derive no comfort from his sister's admonition, "Sorrow is sent by Him, not by man. Men are His instruments, they are not to blame. If you think someone has wronged you, forget it, and forgive! We have no right to punish. And then you will know the happiness of forgiving" (699).

John Hagan sees the attempted elopement of Natasha as an event which brings Prince Andrew to the "nadir of his moral life." In his refusal to forgive Natasha, Andrew's pride comes to the fore, as his retort to Pierre indicates, "I said that a fallen woman should be forgiven, but I didn't say I could forgive her" (661). The "crisis of hatred" continues but five months (January to June 1812), however. In Andrew's rapid recovery Hagan insists that Tolstoy is suggesting the speed with which Andrew is maturing and approaching the climax of his development.[13] Forgiveness comes from suffering, after Borodino.

It is the year 1812, seven years after the battle of Austerlitz, at which time the wounded Andrew lying on the battlefield perceived the insignificance of his hero Napoleon against the background of the infinite sky. On the eve of the battle of Borodino Andrew is thinking of his youthful belief in "ideal love" (858) which was to have kept Natasha faithful to him for a year. Suddenly he remembers that his foe is still alive and happy. Again he is moved by desire for revenge.

During the battle Andrew is wounded by a grenade. At the hospital tent he lies on an operating table adjoining a table on which lies a man whose leg has just been amputated. In that miserable, sobbing, enfeebled man he recognizes Anatole Kuragin. Gradually he recalls that this man is somehow closely associated with his life. The theme of wrath is now to be supplanted by the theme of love.

All at once an unexpected memory of Natasha as he had seen her the night of the ball arouses in his heart a love stronger than ever. Love of a woman will eventually be transmuted into love of the enemy and ultimately into love of Christ. As Andrew observes Anatole, "ecstatic pity and love for that man" overflows his happy heart (908). The wounded Andrew now echoes the Christian precept the author enunciated later in *A Confession* but which permeates much of his earlier work: "Compassion, love of our brothers, for those who love us and for those who hate us, love of our enemies; yes, that love which God preached on earth and which Princess Mary taught me and I did not understand—that is what made me sorry to part with life, that is what remained for me had I lived" (908). At the crisis of death, Tolstoy's Homeric hero of 1807 becomes the Christian hero of 1812. The *Iliad* which Tolstoy so greatly admired is yielding in significance to the Sermon on the Mount.

Meanwhile, as war comes closer to Moscow, the city is being abandoned. The French are occupying the capital; the holy city of the tsars is burning. The Rostovs—their prized possessions packed in carts—are about to leave the city. But Natasha, distressed that so many wounded soldiers must be left behind because of lack of conveyances, instigates the unloading of some of the family's carts to provide vehicles for the wounded. Among the wounded is Andrew, a fact concealed from Natasha as long as possible. The news, however, reaches Natasha on the journey. Subsequently when her attention is called to the awesome sight of the fires burning in Moscow, her thoughts are elsewhere. Dazed by the thought of Andrew's condition, she asks vaguely, "What's burning?" and answers, "Oh, yes, Moscow" (1017). Thereafter at all the halts on the journey and finally at the Rostovs' dwelling at Yaroslavl, Natasha is at Andrew's side nursing him for more than a month during his slow dying of peritonitis.[14] Andrew is about to find in Natasha the woman he had once loved and whose betrayal he has forgiven.

In a respite from delirium Prince Andrew calls for the Gospels. Then he reflects upon the significance of the doctrine of love, the love which he first experienced when he saw his enemy Anatole and loved him. "To love one's neighbors, to love one's enemies, to love everything, to love God in all His manifestations. It is possible to love some one dear to you with human love, but an enemy can only be loved with divine love. . . .

"When loving with human love one may pass from love to hatred, but divine love cannot change. No, neither death nor anything else can destroy it. It is the essence of the soul. Yet how many people have I hated in my life? And of them all, I loved and hated none as I did her" (1023). Prince Andrew pictures to himself Natasha, not as he had known her in the past with her charms that gave him delight, but this time he pictures to himself her soul (1023).[15]

He experiences another period of delirium. When he revives, the living Natasha, whom he most longed to love with the new divine love that has been revealed to him, is on her knees at his side. Thereafter she watches over him during intervals of partial recovery and relapse.

Meanwhile, the more deeply Andrew penetrates into the new principle of eternal love, the more he unconsciously detaches himself from life. At length he understands that "To love everything and everybody and always to sacrifice oneself for love" means "not to love anyone, not to live this earthly life" (1087). The more deeply imbued with this principle he becomes, the more firmly he destroys the barrier which stands between life and death.

Again his love for Natasha awakens. Love for a woman still binds him to life. Here the transition from earthly to supernatural love suggests the Platonic theory of earthly love as the means by which the aspirations of time-bound mortals are led to the contemplation of the eternal, from physical love to the ideal form of divine love. At this stage, Andrew declares he loves Natasha "more than anything in the world." If only he could live, "How good it would be!" he assures her (1089).

This episode is significant because of its autobiographical aspect. It suggests an earlier episode which reveals in

Prince Andrew's nature the discord which was also so much a part of his creator's life. In the earlier episode (512) while Natasha is singing Prince Andrew suddenly feels tears choking him. He feels happy and at the same time sad. "The chief reason," Tolstoy tells us, "was a sudden, vivid sense of the terrible contrast between something infinitely great and illimitable within him and that limited and material something that he, and even she, was." A comment by Simmons is revealing. Simmons writes: "Like Tolstoy, the only thing Prince Andrew was sure about was that there was something precious and unknown within him striving to escape, while the flesh bound him to earth. Only in the remarkable scene of his passing, when he discovered that death was a great awakening, did he get a glimpse of what that something was."[16]

In the final scene Prince Andrew falls asleep brooding upon the opposition between life and death. Now the author in the mouth of his character enunciates the Christian paradox of life in death. Love is life, love hinders death—that Andrew understands because of his earthly love for Natasha. But on the level of the supernatural Andrew perceives, "Love is God, and to die means that I, a particle of love, shall return to the general and eternal source" (1089). These thoughts, however, are confusing; they are too intellectual.

Shortly before his death Prince Andrew surrenders himself emotionally. He dreams that Death has come through a door which he has tried with all his might to keep shut. But at the instant when he is dying he awakes from the terrifying dream. From that day, with awakening from sleep, there began for Prince Andrew an awakening from life. Since the "change" observed by Natasha has come over him, he is aloof from all things earthly.[17] Moreover, as a Christian hero, Prince Andrew has paradoxically found life in death. As Homer's epic became the expression of pagan immortality, Tolstoy's epic becomes the expression of Christian immortality.

With the thought of death Tolstoy had been preoccupied since 1860, when he observed the slow dying of his beloved brother Nikolai as a result of tuberculosis. Tolstoy, who had witnessed thousands of deaths at Sevastopol and elsewhere, tells us that he had noted them only with his "bodily" eyes, but the death of his brother made him see death for the first time with his "spiritual" eyes. He was overcome—helpless before its power. Thereafter the thought of death never left him. Tolstoy's observation of the paradox of life in death, as illustrated in the death of Prince Andrew, foreshadows what some writers are disposed to call the author's spiritual crisis, described in *A Confession,* published more than a decade after the publication of *War and Peace.* In the later work the author explores more deeply moral uncertainties which had perplexed him during the writing of *War and Peace.*

HELENE KURAGINA

We have observed in the partially autobiographical hero, Prince Andrew, the author's effort to reconcile the Greek outlook on life with the teachings of the Gospels— to impose the theme of love upon the theme of wrath—to transform a Homeric archetype into a Christian antitype. One more illustration may serve to distinguish the Homeric archetype from the Tolstoyan antitype. Helen of

Troy, the archetype of a beautiful woman—to Marlowe's Faustus "the face that launched a thousand ships, / And burnt the topless towers of Ilium"—suggests the "beautiful Helene" Kuragina as the author first reveals her to us in *War and Peace*.

The rebirth of a myth in successive epochs in different cultures enables Tolstoy to model Helene initially on the Homeric archetype, but as the author's propensity to judge according to the ethical dualism of Christianity becomes an aesthetic principle, we observe Helene portrayed not as a character in which beauty has a favorable connotation, but as an ambivalent character, and ultimately as a Tolstoyan antitype.

Tolstoy separates his characters into two distinct categories, the good and the bad. Indeed, Tolstoy's favorite thesis, according to Maude, is "What is good and what is bad? With what must we sympathize and what must we reject?" And the reply, continues Maude, is that the "predatory, artificial and insincere types," exemplified by such characters among the Russians as Helene, Anatole, and Dolohov, are repugnant to Tolstoy, "while he loves the humble, the meek and the sincere."[18] The subtle change in the characterization of Helene—one of a family of five, all described unfavorably—is indicative of the author's attitude toward his art.

In contrast to Tolstoy, Homer seldom creates a "bad" character. Even the ancients observed that Homer praises everything. The rhetor Dio of Prusa, hardly conscious of the connection between the praise of merit and the noble style of the epic, describes Homer's ability to exalt everything he touches. "Homer," he says, "praised almost everything—animals and plants, water and earth, weapons and horses. He passed over nothing without somehow honoring and glorifying it. Even the one man whom he abused, Thersites, he called a *clear-voiced speaker.*"[19] The one man Homer describes as ridiculously ugly he redeems, according to the rhetor, in a phrase.

When first described by Tolstoy, the beautiful Helene appears glamorous among her admirers. Later, after numerous ironic repetitions of the epithet "beautiful," we see her as an ambivalent character, particularly in her effort to entice Natasha to Anatole. Ultimately we perceive that Tolstoy views her with more irony than admiration. Beauty no longer corresponds to goodness.

The "beautiful Helene" (7) is introduced walking in the drawing room of her hostess among men who gaze in admiration at the "classic beauty of her figure" (12). Helen of Troy, as she first appears in the third book of the *Iliad,* is seen walking with two handmaidens on the wall of Troy among the old councilors. Though the face of Helen is veiled, the old men praise her beauty. "Small blame is it that Trojans and well-greaved Achaeans should for such a woman suffer hardships: marvellously like is she to the immortal goddesses to look upon" (III, 156–158). Praise enough, when we recall that Achilles too is godlike!

Although Helen and Helene are revealed by the impression they leave on the viewer, we sense rather than see Helen's beauty of form and movement. Her physical features are not described. She is "long-robed Helen, fair among women" (III, 228). Helene, on the other hand, is partially exposed. "With a slight rustle of her white dress trimmed with moss and ivy, with a gleam of white shoulders, glossy hair, and sparkling diamonds, she passed between the men who made way for her, not looking at any of them but smiling on all, as if graciously allowing each the privilege of admiring her beautiful figure and shapely shoulders, back, and bosom—which in the fashion of those days was very much exposed . . ." (11).

But Tolstoy is not satisfied with verbal description, especially of Helene's salient characteristic, her "bust, which had always seemed like marble to Pierre" (222). The artist employed to depict Helene was given careful instructions. In a letter to M. S. Bashilov, who was making a set of illustrations for a private edition of *War and Peace*, the author gave directions for emphasizing certain features. The notation referring to Helene reads:

Helene: Couldn't you make her bustier. (Plastic beauty of forms is her most characteristic trait.)[20]

We observe Helene on her name day through the eyes of her suitor, Pierre, who every day said to himself, "It is time I understood her and made up my mind what she really is. Was I mistaken before, or am I mistaken now? No, she is not stupid, . . . She says little, but what she does say is always clear and simple, so she is not stupid. . . ." Then he concludes, "She was right in regarding all arguments as nonsense in comparison with that smile" (225). At the name-day celebration the beautiful Helene and Pierre, seated side by side, are silent for a long time while the guests wait impatiently for Pierre's proposal. Pierre feels an incomprehensible shame, though he knows he is considered a lucky man, "a sort of Paris possessed of a Helen" (228).[21]

Later in the evening, alone with Helen in the drawing room, Pierre still hesitates to take the final step. "He felt ashamed; he felt that he was occupying someone else's

place here beside Helene" (229). At the opportune moment Helene's father, Prince Vasili, plays the part of Paris
and "abducts" not an unwilling Homeric Helen but the
willing Helene (230). With Helene in his possession,
Pierre can no longer vacillate. As Pierre holds the hand of
his betrothed, looking at her beautiful bosom rise and fall,
he reflects that "something special is always said in such
cases," but he cannot remember what. Again he experiences uncertainty but he tries to control himself. "It is too
late now, it's done; besides I love her." And he remembers what is said on such occasions, *"Je vous aime!"*
(using the formal *vous*) (231). He is now the possessor of "a
celebrated beauty" as well as heir to his father's millions.

The gentle irony with which the author depicts the
bewildered Pierre gives the reader an increasingly unfavorable impression of Helene. Later, suggestion of her
infidelity confirms that impression. To determine who will
possess Helene a duel is arranged between Pierre and
Dolohov, even as in the *Iliad* a duel between Menelaus
and Paris was designed to determine who will possess
Helen. In the *Iliad* Helen and all her wealth are to go as
reward to the victor in the duel between husband and
former husband. The duel, however, is interrupted by the
intervention of the goddess Aphrodite. Aphrodite, who
instigated the Trojan War by abetting the abduction of
Helen, now intervenes to save her favorite, Paris. As in
the Homeric episode, Tolstoy's duel between husband and
lover is indecisive. Although Dolohov, the victim, is
merely injured, the outcome is highly significant in
unmasking the character of Helene.

Homer's Helen, had Menelaus conquered, would have
returned happily to Sparta with her former husband,

whose praise she utters as she chides Paris for cowardice: "Verily it was once thy boast that thou wast a better man than Menelaus—in the might of thine arm and thy spear" (III, 430–431). On the other hand, had Pierre destroyed Dolohov, Helene might more readily have sought another lover. At this juncture, however, Helene can but chide Pierre by comparing him to the notorious gambler Dolohov, "A man who's a better man than you in every way . . ." (344). In the rift that follows, Helene receives from Pierre control over the larger part of his property, and Pierre is now ready to admit to himself that his wife is a "depraved woman" (542, 543).

Two years later Helene implores Pierre to return to her. Now an enthusiastic follower of the rules of Masonry, Pierre concludes that he cannot refuse a suppliant, though union with her will henceforth have only a "spiritual aim" (480). After a sojourn abroad, Helene is now a prominent member of the Petersburg French circle, sympathetic to Napoleon. To be received by Countess Bezukhova is regarded as a "diploma of intellect" (481). Young men read books before attending her evenings; ambassadors confided diplomatic secrets. In the presence of the "most distinguished woman in Petersburg" politics, poetry, and philosophy were discussed, and in Helene's every word everyone looked for a profound meaning "of which she herself had no conception" (482). Her "queer husband" occasionally appeared with the hostess, though he "knew she was very stupid" (482). The barbed irony directed at Helene indicates that Pierre is still the author's spokesman.

A comparison between Helene and Natasha (who will later become Pierre's wife) leaves no doubt of the author's antipathy. Natasha at her first ball is dancing with Prince Andrew. "Her slender bare arms and neck were not beautiful—compared to Helene's her shoulders looked thin and her bosom undeveloped. But Helene seemed, as it were, hardened by a varnish left by the thousands of looks that had scanned her person, while Natasha was like a girl exposed for the first time, who would have felt very much ashamed had she not been assured that this was absolutely necessary" (504–505).

We last observe Helene in a brilliantly ironic episode in which she argues for intimacy with two lovers, an elderly magnate and a young foreign prince, though Pierre is legally her husband. Helene is willing to marry both, lest she disappoint either. Those few in her intimate circle who see in her proposal a "desecration of the sacrament of marriage" remain silent. Only Marya Dmitrievna Akhrosimova expresses a contrary opinion. Meeting Helene at a ball, she speaks in her gruff voice, amid general silence: "So wives of living men have started marrying again! Perhaps you think you have invented a novelty? You have been forestalled, my dear! It was thought of long ago. It is done in all the brothels" (935). But Marya Dmitrievna in Petersburg society is regarded as a buffoon. We recall that King Lear's fool also uttered authorial wisdom.

La Belle Helene, at first partially exposed, is gradually stripped by the author until she stands naked to the world. Her ubiquitous smile (11, 22, 225, 622, and elsewhere) no longer conceals her character. She dies as the result of an abortion, after entrusting herself to an Italian doctor whose cure consists in removing an "inconvenience" (1038). A fitting epitaph might be the words of Napoleon who, during the famous meeting of the Emperors at Erfurt, had noticed Helene in the theater and remarked, *"C'est un superbe animal"* (481). Like Napoleon, the poseur, Helene seeks exemption from the burden of moral law. In the eyes of the author, both are, to use his denigrating phrase, superb beasts.

Chapter III

HISTORY TO MYTH

HELENE, as a fictional character, Tolstoy was justified in rejecting as "bad," but inclusion of an historical character, Napoleon, in the same category poses
questions of the author's credibility. In like manner, the
transformation of the historical Kutuzov, from a leader not
without human frailties to a hero corresponding to the
author's own conception of the "good," poses further questions of the attainment of "truth." Yet, writes Tolstoy in a
draft for the introduction to *War and Peace*, "I was afraid
that the necessity to describe important personages of
1812 would force me to be guided by historical documents
rather than by the truth."[1] Tolstoy is intent upon amend-
ing the pages of history by challenging the views of historians. He is creating his own "myths" in accord with the
dualism of Christianity.

Homer, on the other hand, is interested not in challenging the falsehood of historians but in telling an artistic
truth in poetic form. Aristotle praises Homer for this
attribute: "It is Homer who has chiefly taught other poets
the art of telling lies skillfully."[2] Yet for that very art early
Greek historians denounce Homer. Herodotus had little
regard for the poet as historian. Writing about four hundred years after Homer, Herodotus accuses the poet of
deliberately telling lies; and Thucydides, writing in the
same century, during the Peloponessian War, concurs in
that low opinion of Homer as historian.[3]

Nevertheless, belief in the historicity of epic poetry was
alive in the time of Herodotus and Thucydides, who re-

garded Homer's epics as history even though they challenged their veracity. The opinion of Herodotus, implicit in the early chapters of his history, becomes explicit in the discussion of the Trojan War.[4] Homer knew what had happened to Helen in Egypt but for the purpose of epic poetry he preferred his own version.[5] Herodotus relates that violent winds drove Paris, absconding with Helen, from the Aegean sea into the Egyptian sea, whence he came to Egypt. Proteus, ruler of Memphis, detained Helen, with all her wealth, to await the coming of Menelaus, while he sent Paris back to Troy.[6] Herodotus continues, "This, by what the priests told me, was the manner of Helen's coming to Proteus. And, to my thinking, Homer too knew this story; but seeing that it suited not so well with epic poetry as the tale of which he made use, he rejected it of set purpose; . . ."[7] Herodotus concludes his account in this fashion: Menelaus demands of the Trojans restitution of Helen and her possessions, but the Trojans deny she is with them. The Greeks think the Trojans mock them and therewith besiege the city, capture it, and find no Helen. Menelaus then goes to Proteus, who restores Helen unharmed.[8]

In defence of Homer, we have the authority of Aristotle to tell us that poetry is more significant than history because it aims at the universal while history is concerned with the particular. Aristotle insists that "it is not the function of the poet to relate what has happened, but what may happen,—what is possible according to the law of probability or necessity. The poet and the historian differ not by writing in verse or in prose. The work of Herodotus might be put into verse, and it would still be a species of history, with metre no less than without it. The true difference is that one relates what has happened, the other what may happen. Poetry, therefore, is a more philosophical and higher thing than history: for poetry tends to express the universal, history the particular. By the universal I mean how a person of a certain type will on occasion speak or act, according to the law of probability or necessity; . . ."⁹

When we examine Tolstoy's "philosophy of history" it will become apparent that the author is seeking to justify what Aristotle calls "probable impossibilities." Tolstoy's denigration of Napoleon and his apotheosis of Kutuzov may serve as examples of poetic treatment Aristotle defends when he asserts, "With respect to the requirements of art, a probable impossibility is to be preferred to a thing improbable and yet possible."¹⁰ Nevertheless, in his deliberate effort to tell the truth, Tolstoy is more like the peasant poet Hesiod than like Homer, for Hesiod in his *Works and Days* vows that he will tell his brother the truth. Homer, on the other hand, states the purpose of epic poetry dispassionately in the words of Helen addressing Hector in the *Iliad*: "Zeus bringeth evil doom, that even in days to come we may be a song in the ears of men that shall be hereafter" (VI, 357–358). To Homer myth is history, and epic is the poet's mouthpiece. In Tolstoy's hands, history becomes "myth."

NAPOLEON

In the characterization of Napoleon, Tolstoy is concerned with the relation of power to goodness. Must the "great" men be first and foremost a good man? Tolstoy would answer in the affirmative, for he will not allow us to burke the vexed question of the historian's attitude toward moral judgment. Since Tolstoy's favorite thesis, if we give credence to his biographer Maude, poses the question, "What is good and what is bad?" it becomes increasingly evident that the author introduces a scale of values in human relations such as we need not seek in Homer.

"Napoleon le Grande!" the world has been repeating for fifty years. *"C'est grand!"* say the historians, with the result that "there no longer exists either good or evil but only *'grand'* and 'not *grand.'* *Grand* is good, not *grand* is bad. *Grand* is the characteristic, in their conception, of some special animals called 'heroes.' " (1187).

Repeatedly Tolstoy depicts the *grand* Napoleon as a poseur. When the author refers to his chief target, we cannot fail to observe his use of the sharp weapon of irony. It is the irony of a man whose emotions are so strong he cannot trust himself on the flood of them.

We observe the French Emperor as he awaits a Russian delegation to welcome him to Moscow. Napoleon is observing Moscow from a nearby hill. The strange city lies at his feet like an Oriental beauty about to be ravished. He reflects upon his power. "One word from me, one movement of my hand, and that ancient capital of the Tsars would perish" (972). But as conqueror he will be magnanimous; he will spare her. After the victory he will be a beneficent ruler: "On the ancient monuments of barbarism and despotism I will inscribe the great words of justice and mercy" (972). He waits for the observance of proprieties, a deputation from the Tsar to receive him. Then he becomes impatient. He gives a sign with his hand and after a single report from a signaling gun the invading army marches into Moscow. Though half the population

64

remains in Moscow, the city is deserted. "It was empty in the sense that a dying queenless hive is empty," writes Tolstoy (794). When with due circumspection Napoleon is informed of the unexpected situation, he says to himself, "Moscow deserted! What an incredible event!" (976) His actor's instinct has misled him. His *coup de théatre* has not come off.

This is Napoleon the impostor. Tolstoy describes him in four vituperative epic similes. In a simile Tolstoy pictures Napoleon before the battle of Borodino as an insolent surgeon exulting in his power. On the eve of the momentous event Napoleon jokes and chats carelessly, "as a famous, self-confident surgeon who knows his job does when turning up his sleeves and putting on his apron while a patient is being strapped to the operating table. "The matter is in my hands and is clear and definite in my head. When the time comes to set to work I shall do it as no one else could, but now I can jest, and the more I jest and the calmer I am the more tranquil and confident you ought to be, and the more amazed at my genius' " (877).

During the course of the battle, the expected success having eluded him, Napoleon realizes that "the terrible stroke of his arm had supernaturally become impotent" (896). Since he lacked power to stop the useless slaughter, the conflict "for the first time, seemed to him unnecessary and horrible" (898). Like an unlucky gambler, the Emperor appears in another simile. "Napoleon was experiencing a feeling of depression like that of an ever-lucky gambler who, after recklessly flinging money about and always winning, suddenly just when he has calculated all the chances of the game, finds that the more he considers his play the more surely he loses" (896).

After describing the battle of Borodino, which Tolstoy insists was a moral victory for his countrymen, and after exposing the futility of the pillage of Moscow, the author reveals in two brief similes the vainglorious Emperor shorn of his fantastic power. Napoleon's impotence, which the world mistook for power, now seems "as the figurehead of a ship may seem to a savage to guide the vessel" (1118). He is powerless as "a child who, holding a couple of strings inside a carriage, thinks he is driving it" (1118). Nevertheless, historians insist upon calling him a great genius. Tolstoy parodies the view of historians:

> At that time there was in France a man of genius—Napoleon. He conquered everybody everywhere—that is, he killed many people because he was a great genius. And for some reason he went to kill Africans, and killed them so well and was so cunning and wise that when he returned to France he ordered everybody to obey him, and they all obeyed him. Having become an Emperor he again went out to kill people in Italy, Austria, and Prussia. And there too he killed a great many. In Russia there was an Emperor, Alexander, who decided to restore order in Europe and therefore fought against Napoleon. In 1807 he suddenly made friends with him, but in 1811 they again quarreled and again began killing many people. Napoleon led six hundred thousand men into Russia and captured Moscow; then he suddenly ran away from Moscow, and the Emperor Alexander, helped by the advice of Stein and others, united Europe to arm against the disturber of its peace. All Napoleon's allies suddenly became his enemies and their forces advanced against the fresh forces he raised. The Allies defeated Napoleon, entered Paris, forced Napoleon to abdicate, and sent him to the island of Elba, not depriving him of the title of Emperor and showing him every respect,

*though five years before and one year later they all
regarded him as an outlaw and a brigand. (1315–1316)*

Finally, as Tolstoy revealed Helene shorn of her beauty,
he now exposes to the audience the actor Napoleon
deprived of his mask. The last role has been played. The
actor's histrionics have ended. The impostor is about to
make his exit—but not without a bow to his Creator.

*The actor is bidden to disrobe and wash off his powder and
paint: he will not be wanted any more.*

*And some years pass during which he plays a pitiful
comedy to himself in solitude on his island, justifying his
actions by intrigues and lies when the justification is no
longer needed, and displaying to the whole world what it
was that people had mistaken for strength so long as an
unseen hand directed his actions.*

*The manager having brought the drama to a close and
stripped the actor shows him to us.*

*"See what you believed in! This is he! Do you now see
that it was not he but I who moved you?" (1262)*

We have observed the author's emphasis on moral values,
in both fiction and fact; in the depiction of two of his
fictional characters, Prince Andrew and Helene Kuragina,
and in his depiction of the historical Napoleon. These
characters the author praises and condemns in accordance
with his own rigid standard of morality. It thus becomes
evident that Tolstoy is the inheritor of a very long
tradition which has its roots in Palestine. He states his
standard for judgment in *War and Peace:* "For us with the
standard of good and evil given us by Christ, no human
actions are incommensurable. And there is no greatness
where simplicity, goodness, and truth are absent" (1187).

67

KUTUZOV

In the example of Napoleon the author has illustrated his conception of a man called by historians a "great" hero. In the example of Kutuzov he illustrates his conception of a hero truly great, according to his own standard of excellence, "simplicity, goodness, and truth." Kutuzov is a leading example of Tolstoy's "heroism of meekness." According to the critic Strakhov, who assisted the author in preparation of his 1873 edition, Tolstoy is the poet who glorifies the meek hero.[11]

Strakhov continues, "The aim of the whole story of *War and Peace* is to prove the superiority of meek heroism over active heroism."[12] Tolstoy himself places Kutuzov in the category of the meek hero when he insists, "That simple, modest, and therefore truly great, figure could not be cast in the false mold of a European hero—the supposed ruler of men—that history has invented" (1208). Strakhov concludes that the author "has given us a new Russian formula for the heroic life."[13] He has given us, according to Strakhov, "an epic in a contemporary form of art."[14]

As hero of a new type of epic, Kutuzov is given a definite role to play, a role directly opposite to that of the impostor Napoleon. Tolstoy intends to rectify the errors of historians by emphasizing Kutuzov's service to his country. Love of country is Kutuzov's dominant characteristic, and in this respect he may be compared to Hector, who represents a more advanced conception of *arete*—that a man fulfills himself better in the service of his country than does Achilles, who satisfies his own honor.

Tolstoy insists that it was recognition of Kutuzov's "national feeling" (1208) which led the people to select

him—contrary to the Tsar's wish—to be their representative in a national war. Kutuzov thus becomes the
representative of the heroic Russian populace, a stellar
example of the unconscious spirit of the Russian nation.

At this point a comment by Bowra is pertinent: "When
a country is under foreign domination, there is a tendency
for every man to become a hero who resists or fights the
conqueror."[15] Likewise, Tolstoy asserts that understanding
of history begins not with the examination of "great" men's
deeds, but with the study of an infinitely large number of
infinitely small actions, those of the unsung heroes who
represent the unconscious spirit of the nation. Strakhov
lists Tolstoy's heroes: "In general, the whole mass of our
soldiers and the Russian people belong to the category of
meek heroism, including Tushin, Timokhin, Dokhturov,
Konovnitsen, and Kutuzov himself, the best example."[16]

Here it might be interjected that although Tolstoy
celebrates the acts of heroism of obscure men who did not
pretend to influence the course of history, he also
remembers not only Kutuzov but other leaders neglected
or ridiculed by historians. He insists that the generals
Dokhturov (1131) and Konovnitsen (1134) seem "to have
been included merely for propriety's sake in the list of the
so-called heroes of 1812." Tolstoy gives them a more
exalted position when, using the epic simile, he compares
them to cogwheels which without clatter constitute the
most essential part of the machine (1134).

As chief of Tolstoy's "meek" heroes, Kutuzov is praised
by Prince Andrew, who serves under the commander as a
staff officer: "He understands that there is something
stronger and more important than his own will—the
inevitable course of events, and he can see them and grasp

their significance, and seeing that significance can refrain from meddling and renounce his personal wish directed to something else" (831).

Moreover, Prince Andrew believes in him "because he's Russian." Here we observe Tolstoy the Slavophile speaking and concluding the eulogy with his own comment, "On such feelings, more or less dimly shared by all, the unanimity and general approval were founded with which, despite court influences, the popular choice of Kutuzov as commander in chief was received" (831).

In the role which the author has given Kutuzov to play, the commander in chief is stripped of his more unfavorable characteristics, some of which appear in the drafts but not in the final version. In the final version the author defends his hero: "Kutuzov is described by foreigners as a crafty, dissolute, weak old courtier, and by Russians as something indefinite—a sort of puppet useful only because he has a Russian name" (1205). Such, says Tolstoy, is the fate of those rare individuals who "discerning the will of Providence, submit their personal will to it" (1205). In the final version we see Tolstoy the moralist at work rather than Tolstoy the historian, as he creates a mythical hero.

The historical Kutuzov (1745–1813) was hardly a meek hero. By the year 1805, the year in which *War and Peace* begins, he had already enjoyed a great military reputation. He had taken part in the Turkish war in Catherine's reign, where he proved to be, like Suvorov, an attacking general. During the campaign he had been seriously injured and had lost an eye, a fact remembered by Tolstoy when, in an episode in *War and Peace*, the commander is about to send his men into a disastrous battle. The comment comes from the lips of Prince Andrew, "Yes, he has a right to speak so calmly of those men's death," Prince Andrew reflects, as he glances at Kutuzov's empty eye socket (180).

Later, as Governor-General of Petersburg, Kutuzov had displeased the Emperor, Alexander I. Hence he had been living for three years in disfavor in the country. He had been recalled in 1805 to lead an army of fifty thousand men to the aid of Austria.[17]

As a "meek" hero, the man who knows he cannot lead stands in contrast to the man who thinks he is leading. As represented by Tolstoy, the Russian commander, whose impassivity is a logical policy, is guided by events upon which he does not seek to impose his will. Yet there is no doubt that the symbolically impassive Kutuzov acts, that his decisions influence the course of events. The chief decision Kutuzov makes in the national war is the decision to abandon Moscow to the enemy, for, says Tolstoy, "He alone said the loss of Moscow was not the loss of Russia" (1207). Having listened apathetically to conflicting arguments of generals at the Council of War, Kutuzov pronounces the final words which seal the fate of Moscow:

> *Gentlemen, I have heard your views. Some of you will not*
> *agree with me. But I . . . by the authority entrusted to me*
> *by my Sovereign and country, order a retreat. (927–928)*

This is the Old Cuncator (277) whose motto is "Patience and Time" (1207), *"tout vient à celui qui sait attendre,"* the man who achieved the aim toward which he exerted all his power, "not to slaying and destroying men but to saving and showing pity on them" (1208). He is the meek hero who refused to sacrifice the lives not only of his own men but also of the French invaders. When, having burned and looted Moscow, the starving half-frozen troops of Napoleon abandoned the city, the Kutuzov of Tolstoy's epic is moved by compassion. He utters his feelings when, speaking like "an ordinary old man" (1210), he bids farewell to his troops:

> You see, brothers, I know it's hard for you, but it can't be helped! Bear up, it won't be for long now! We'll see our visitors off and then we'll rest. The Tsar won't forget your service. It is hard for you, but still you are at home while they—you see what they have come to. . . . Worse off than our poorest beggars. While they were strong we didn't spare ourselves, but now we may even pity them. They are human beings too. Isn't it so, lads? (1210)

Here Kutuzov appears as the meek hero whom Tolstoy has invented to support his philosophy of history.

In an essay "Lev Tolstoy's Historical Scepticism" Isaiah Berlin contends that Tolstoy seems almost deliberately to ignore the historical facts in order to bolster his thesis. Berlin writes: "The character of Kutuzov is a case in point. Such heroes as Pierre Bezukhov or Karataev are at least imaginary, and Tolstoy had an undisputed right to endow them with all the attributes he admired. . . . But Kutuzov was a real person, and it is all the more instructive to observe the steps by which he transforms him from the sly, elderly, feeble voluptuary, the corrupt and somewhat sycophantic courtier of the early drafts of War and Peace, which were based on authentic sources, into the unforgettable symbol of the Russian people in all its simplicity and intuitive wisdom. By the time we reach the celebrated passage—one of the most moving in literature—in which Tolstoy describes the moment when the old man is woken in his camp at Fili to be told that the French army is retreating, we have left the facts behind us, and are in an imaginary realm, an historical and emotional atmosphere for which the evidence is flimsy, but which is artistically indispensable to Tolstoy's design. The final apotheosis of Kutuzov is wholly unhistorical for all Tolstoy's repeated profession of his undeviating devotion to the sacred cause of truth" (1138).[18] In Tolstoy's democracy of heroism the leader Kutuzov has undergone a metamorphosis from the truth of history to the more poetic truth of art.

As we have seen, both Kutuzov and Napoleon are mythical figures pitted one against the other. From time immemorial authors have used the technique of parallel contrasts, pairing opposing male characters, one as a foil for the other. Commonly the characters are locked in male friendship, as are Achilles and Patroclus in Homer and Aeneas and Achates in Virgil. Immediately other relationships come to mind, the Biblical friendship of David and Jonathan and the knight-squire relationship of Don Quixote and Sancho. There are Hamlet and his foil Horatio, who is not passion's slave, and Dostoevsky's Raskolnikov (who early aspires to become a Napoleonic superman) and his friend Razumihin, voice of reason.

Tolstoy is using a similar fictional technique when he creates Kutuzov and Napoleon, but Tolstoy, in his use of antithetical parallels, carries the device a step further. He uses it to enunciate a thesis. Instead of representing a pair of friends who complement each other, Tolstoy depicts a pair of foes, a hero Kutuzov and an antihero Napoleon. In the end, the mythical Kutuzov has been transformed while the mythical Napoleon has been transmogrified, and history has been rewritten.

PHILOSOPHY OF HISTORY

At the heart of Tolstoy's arguments in his philosophy of history lies the problem of fate versus freedom of the will. To the casual reader it may seem as though the disputations of men like Tolstoy, engaged in discussions of this nature, are like soldiers in a stage army marching forever before us; but to the more careful observer it will become apparent that these forces are, in truth, marshalled each time in a new formation and dispatched for a different purpose.

Homer, like Tolstoy, is concerned with the problem of fate (μοῖρα), though he does not think of fate as opposed to freedom of will. Homer commonly illustrates the actions of gods and men as enunciating the power of fate. Ares is ready to take vengeance for the death of a son slain in battle, but Athena stays his wrath, concluding with the understatement, "A hard thing it is to save the lineage and offspring of all men" (IV, 140–141). Here Homer emphasizes the limitation of Olympian power. Beyond the gods stands fate, *moira*.

Homer ultimately explains an incomprehensible event by attributing the cause to fate, of which the gods are interpreters. Thus at a crucial moment in Achilles' life Hera explains the action: "All we from Olympus are come down to mingle in this fight that he take no hurt among the Trojans on this day—afterward he shall suffer whatsoever things Fate span for him with her thread, at his beginning, when his mother bare him" (XX, 125–128). Achilles has his predetermined fate. Achilles will die on his appointed day (αἴσιμον ἦμαρ). So, too, will Hector, who assures his wife Andromache, "No man against my fate shall hurl me to Hades; only destiny, I ween, no man hath

74

escaped, be he coward or be he valiant, when once he hath been born" (VI, 487–489). When Zeus, the dispenser of good and evil, weighs the lot of Hector against that of Achilles in his golden scales (XXII, 209–213), the poet is not suggesting that the fate of Hector is in doubt. Hector's fate has already been decided; the scales serve to dramatize the necessary evil the supernatural powers permit. But it does not occur to Homer to deny his heroes freedom of choice: throughout the *Iliad* all are free agents, for divine foreknowledge of certain events does not imply that all human actions are predetermined.

Homer's *moira* is inscrutable. Although it governs a man's life from the day of his birth, it may be known only in retrospect, after his death. It is also inexorable—witness the destruction of Aegisthus who has gone ὑπὲρ μόρον, *beyond* fate.[19] In the *Odyssey* the transgression of Aegisthus cautions men not to emphasize the supremacy of a supernatural power at the expense of man's power to act; in other words, not to confuse the tragic condition with the tragic process, for, as Frye explains, "Fate, in a tragedy, normally becomes external to the hero only *after* the tragic process has been set going. The Greek *anake* or *moira* is in the normal, or pre-tragic, form the internal balancing condition of life. It appears as external or antithetical necessity only after it has been violated as a condition of life, just as justice is the internal condition of an honest man, but the external antagonist of the criminal."[20]

In Homeric epic the most advanced idea of fate is found in the first book of the *Odyssey*, where Zeus cites the exemplum of Orestes to establish a pattern for the moral problem of retribution. Zeus, presiding over the council of the gods, justifies the ways of god to man by referring to the unbreakable relation between destiny and human error. "Look you now, how ready mortals are to blame the gods. It is from us, they say, that evils come, but they even of themselves, through their own blind folly, have sorrows beyond that which is ordained" (*Odyssey*, I, 31–34).[21] Though this advanced concept may have been imposed on previous versions of the traditional saga of Odysseus, it is nevertheless highly significant as an early explanation of the problem of human suffering. Homer recognizes human responsibility for the blind passions which induce man to err. This early effort of the Greeks to realize the problem of destiny culminated in the maxim of Heraclitus, ἦθος ἀνθρώπῳ δαίμον (character is destiny), but the first step was taken by the poet who created the character of Achilles in the *Iliad*.

In the *Iliad*, Zeus, the viceregent of fate, is generally regarded as an amoral deity. He dispenses good and bad gifts capriciously from the two urns which stand on his threshold.[22] The man to whom he gives a mixture meets sometimes with good fortune, sometimes with evil; he to whom Zeus gives only evil gifts encounters only misfortune: he is honored by neither gods nor men (XXIV, 527–533).[23]

It must be emphasized, however, that Homer's portrayal of the gods is not consistent. Although Zeus in the *Iliad* is seldom represented as an ethical force defending justice, the highest expression of such power is shown in the *Patrocleia* where the poet describes in a notable simile the father of gods and men sending storms from heaven when men distort justice on earth (XVI, 384–393). Disturbances in the moral order are echoed in the natural order. Again, Homer depicts Zeus in wrath, wreaking vengeance against men who give crooked judgments in the agora and drive justice out. In the course of the centuries Zeus continued to embody higher and higher ethical ideals, until in the sixth century he occupied the forefront of the Greek pantheon.[24] A century later Platonic philosophy held as a necessary tenet the belief that Zeus was just, but the seeds of such doctrine had been planted in Homeric epic.

We have dwelt at length on Homer's conception of fate because Tolstoy, after adducing a number of arguments for both fate and freedom of the will, arrives at the imponderable conclusion of the ancients when he affirms, "We are forced to fall back on fatalism as an explanation of irrational events (that is to say, events the reasonableness of which we do not understand)" (669). Nevertheless, the author bases his philosophy of history on the distinction between fate and freedom of the will, and even though the problem will admit of no simple and perhaps no metaphysical solution, we cannot ignore Tolstoy's unremitting attempt to discover the "fatal" first cause, the cause of all causes, especially of the holocaust of 1812, so influential in shaping his country's destiny.

The philosophy of history, expressed in passages commonly called digressions, appears intermittently in part or the whole of the following books: seven, nine, ten, eleven, thirteen, fourteen, and the two epilogues. These passages have aroused considerable controversy among critics; some justify their inclusion, others dissent. Paul Debreczeny argues for the unity of "the private and the public" in that the tension between contradictory ideas of freedom and necessity produces a work "half-epic, half-novel."[25] Boris Eikhenbaum also regards these passages as characteristic of epic style. "An examination of the novel from

this stylistic point of view convinces us that the philosophical, historical digressions were introduced by Tolstoy
really as elements of genre, as a sign of the epic, analogous
to the digressions of the *Iliad*."[26]

R. F. Christian dissents. "From an artistic point of view
there is little to be said for the digressions. It is, I think,
reading too much into them to regard them as genre
elements, as indications of an alleged transition from a
family novel to an epic."[27]

About these passages Maude inquired and received the
author's reply. "He told me he considered the defect of
the book, besides its length, to be the intrusion of a philosophic argument into the story. He still holds the opinions
he held when he wrote it, as to the influence or impotence
of 'great' men, as well as all that he then said about
destiny and free will, but he now realizes that his novel
would have been a better novel without these abstract
disquisitions."[28]

With no intent to digress on the subject of digressions,
let us suggest the origin of certain seemingly extraneous
episodes in the *Iliad* and then compare the function in
Homeric epic with the function in *War and Peace*. Generally the "catalogue of the ships" (II, 484–487) is considered a digression. Here Homer lists the famous warriors on both sides. The list is introduced by an invocation
to the Muse. Memory, whose daughters are the Muses,
will recall to the men of Homer's time the names of their
illustrious ancestors. Here lies the truth of tradition
regarded as history.

Let us take another example. Achilles is inconsolable
after the death of Patroclus. His mother Thetis hears his
cry, as she sits in the depths of the sea, and answers, and

all the sea nymphs, beating their breasts, join in the lament. (XVIIII, 39–49) The list of the Nereids, whose very names are poetry, are catalogued by Homer. Here we have a lament, one of the sources of early epic poetry as it emerges from its mythical origin.

Episodes such as these seem to be the source of heroic lays, which when artfully combined yield epic poetry. As has been observed, the usual heroic poem is quite short since it deals with a single event. It is clear from the songs of Phemius and Demodocus that the short lay relates a single episode. Such an art seems to lie behind the composition of the *Iliad*, in which we find many episodes which once may have been tales complete in themselves.[29] Such are the *aristeiai*, tales of prowess, which reveal the heroism of other leaders while the chief hero, Achilles, is off the scene. Lesser men are thus allowed to display their valor: in single combat, Diomedes (V), Agamemnon (XI), Menelaus (XVII); and in duels, Menelaus against Paris (III), Diomedes against Aeneas (VI), and Ajax against Hector (VII). Several other scenes complete in themselves might once have been separate lays, scenes less intimately associated with warfare, such as the episode of guest-friendship in which the bonds of hospitality bridge several generations to unite the adversaries Glaucus and Diomedes, the scene of the parting of Hector and Andromache, as well as the funeral games celebrated in memory of Patroclus. Indeed, the funeral games are peacetime *aristeiai*, in which warriors lay aside their weapons to vie with one another in athletic contests.

Tolstoy, too, has what may be called *aristeiai*, notably the several scenes of the hunt: the wolf hunt (543–553), the fox hunt and the coursing of the hare (553–559). In the hunt as in warfare, Nicholas Rostov is one of the leading participants. Nicholas, a keen sportsman, sees battle in terms of the hunt. Experiencing his baptism of fire, he runs from an encounter with the French, meanwhile thinking: "Who are they? Why are they running? Can they be coming at me? And why? To kill me? *Me* whom everyone is so fond of?" (201) In consternation Nicholas seizes his pistol and, instead of firing, flings it at the oncoming Frenchman and runs in the other direction like "a hare fleeing from the hounds." (201)

Like the Homeric funeral games, Tolstoy's scenes of the hunt epitomize war on a smaller scale, but in *War and Peace* scenes such as these serve a thematic rather than a structural purpose. Both Homer and Tolstoy are aware that rivalry in close relationship may reveal human motives more powerfully than mass encounters of opposing armies, but Tolstoy carries the device a step further to emphasize moral overtones. In the description of the coursing of the hare, the author indicates that the exploits of the common man may equal those of the aristocrat. In this scene Rugay, "Uncle's" unpromising red borzoi, urged on by her excited owner, is competing with dogs worth thousands of rubles and villages of serfs. Rugay seizes the coveted quarry. "Uncle" dismounts, cuts off a muddy pad of the hare, and throws it to the victorious Rugay. Having looked round as if all were "his enemies," and "with an air of not wishing to speak to anyone," "Uncle" mounts his bay and rides off. Rugay walks along behind "Uncle's" horse "with the serene air of a conqueror." Much later, when "Uncle" rides up to Nicholas— who has now regained his former affectation of indifference—and begins talking to him, Nicholas feels flattered that "Uncle" deigns to speak with him. Here we see the aristocrats on horseback, but we see also the triumph not only of the common man but also of the common dog (555–559).

We have noted the tendency of epic to grow from separate tales. It is important also to observe that Homer in the *Iliad* has succeeded in creating a unity of many disparate elements. Homer might conceivably have been satisfied to compose an *Achilleid*, recounting only the exploits of the chief hero, Achilles, and ending his story with Achilles' death, an event frequently foretold in the *Iliad*. Instead, Homer chose to write of the *wrath* of Achilles, a single theme about which the action of the epic revolves. The uniqueness of the *Iliad* lies in the combination of a number of episodes to form a unity of action showing all the illustrious heroes as participants in one great *aristeia,* terminating in the combat between Achilles and Hector, and with the death of Hector closing the wrath theme.

Bowra discovers that the *Iliad* is organized roughly into three main parts, preceded by a prologue and concluded by an epilogue.[30] The first book he considers the prologue, telling how the wrath of Achilles begins. The first section (II–VIII) tells how the Achaeans try to carry on battle without Achilles and, in spite of the efforts of other heroes, fail. The second section (IX–XV) shows how the Achaean leaders, having failed in their effort to persuade Achilles to return to battle, carry on without him and meet greater reverses. The third section (XVI–XXII) tells how Achilles, seeing the endangered ships, begins to relent and sends Patroclus into battle, and, after Patroclus' death, enters battle himself and slays Hector. The last two books, the epilogue, reveal a mollified Achilles honoring Patroclus in funeral games and displaying his compassion for Priam who has come to ransom the body of his son. With the declaration of a truce to allow time for burial of Hector, the *Iliad* closes. Achilles' wrath has been allayed. The tale has ended.

Significantly, Homer has omitted the account of the nine years' siege of Troy preceding the conclusive tenth year, and although the epic is called an *Iliad*, he has omitted the account of the fall of Ilium. That Achilles will die and that Troy will fall we know, but these events are irrelevant, they are not connected with the theme of wrath. About extraneous matters Homer, unlike the poets of the cyclic epics, had the wisdom to be silent. Aristotle praises Homer for representing in his epic as nearly as possible a single action.[31] Like an organism, the *Iliad* has a beginning, a middle, and an end. Structurally it is linear.

In contrast, the structure of *War and Peace* is cyclical. The end implies a new beginning. Tolsoy suggests that peace is but an interlude between two acts of war. He suggests, furthermore, that in the course of time the vanquished will become the victor and the victor, in turn, will be obliged to defend himself against a future enemy. Thus, as victor, the aged Kutuzov dies. He has represented the Russian people in the movement of the masses from west to east. He cannot anticipate a war turning west, as turn it will, with a new leader. And does not Tolstoy imply that the fictional son of Prince Andrew, reading Plutarch and dreaming of his father's exploits, may eventually become a new leader? He will fulfill the pledge to his father in the next generation and will "do something with which even *he* would be satisfied . . ." (1309). Here the lacuna at the end of the first epilogue indicates that, as in Joyce's *Finnegans Wake*, the flow of events is onward.[32] The river of time will, in a cyclical movement, return humanity for replenishment to its source.

The circular movement suggests also the author's paradoxical logic in his unremitting quest for the cause of an event, particularly the War of 1812. Late in life, in the *Confession*, his probing led him to conclude, "I know that the explanation of everything, like the commencement of everything, must be concealed in infinity. But I wish to understand in a way which will bring me to what is inevitably inexplicable."

In *War and Peace* the author, persisting in an effort to understand, continues to assail the bastions of the historians. Historians have rejected the "fate" of the ancients working through the will of a divine leader for a predestined end but have replaced the beliefs of the ancients with no new conceptions, argues Tolstoy (1314). Couching his argument in mathematical terms in the hope that such rational demonstration will prove irrefutable, he offers the example of Achilles and the tortoise to show the fallacy of the argument of historians who take smaller and smaller arbitrary units in an effort to explain events.

Tolstoy insists that "to take any unit disconnected from others, or to assume a beginning of any phenomenon, or to say that the will of many men is expressed by the actions of any one historic personage" is false (918). Only by taking infinitesimally small units and integrating them can we arrive at the laws of history. The race between Achilles and the tortoise, rightly interpreted, illustrates the principle governing continuous motion.

FROM ACHILLES TO CHRIST

There is a well-known, so-called sophism of the ancients consisting in this, that Achilles could never catch up with a tortoise he was following, in spite of the fact that he travelled ten times as fast as the tortoise. By the time Achilles has covered the distance that separated him from the tortoise, the tortoise has covered one tenth of that distance ahead of him: when Achilles has covered that tenth, the tortoise has covered another one hundredth, and so on forever. This problem seemed to the ancients insoluble. The absurd answer (that Achilles could never overtake the tortoise) resulted from this: that motion was arbitrarily divided into discontinuous elements, whereas the motion both of Achilles and of the tortoise was continuous. (917)

In the continuity of events flowing from the first cause Tolstoy discovers the victory of 1812. To the morale of the men in the ranks, to the common soldiers, and ultimately to the unconscious spirit of the Russian people he attributes most of the success in war, resulting in 1812 in what he chooses to call the moral victory of Borodino and the deferred victory following the loss of Moscow. The people, the *narod*, are his unsung heroes of history, yet historians insist upon attributing the cause of events to the will of their leaders. Standing as the common men do at the base of the ladder of influence, their involuntary actions are more nearly related to the first cause than are the voluntary actions of all the celebrated leaders who stand on the top rung of the ladder. Hence, to attribute the cause of an event to the deeds of the leader is fallacious because "The actions of Napoleon and Alexander, on whose words the event seemed to hang, were as little voluntary as the actions of any soldier who was drawn into the campaign by lot or by conscription" (669).

84

Now Tolstoy utters his famous dictum, "A king is history's slave" (670). Why? Because "Man lives consciously for himself, but is an unconscious instrument in the attainment of the historic, universal aims of humanity. A deed done is irrevocable, and its result coinciding in time with the actions of millions of other men assumes an historic significance. The higher a man stands on the social scale, the more people he is connected with and the more power he has over others, the more evident is the predestination and inevitability of his every action" (670).

If Tolstoy places too much emphasis on the impotence of "great" men, if he stresses too strongly their lack of freedom of action, his argument shows the greater strength of his offensive over his defensive attack. In an effort to demonstrate the truth of his statement, "A king is history's slave," he offers examples of military commanders like Napoleon, who, as a horse in a treadmill, fulfills a predestined role (909) in a war likened to moves in a game of chess (877). Nor does he spare generals in the Russian army: the German general Pfuel, with his dogmatic theories, represents the worst traits of all the strategists on paper—he feels most at home sitting down in front of a map (709). Besides Pfuel, the Russian generals with alien names, who regard war as a rational enterprise, include Benningsen, Toll, Barclay de Tolly, and Wintzengerode.

Such superfluous leaders the author contrasts with Kutuzov who, apprehending the spirit of the army, attempts to guide his forces without imposing his will. "By long years of military experience he knew, and with the wisdom of age understood, that it is impossible for one man to direct hundreds of thousands of others struggling with death, and he knew that the result of a battle is decided not by the orders of a commander in chief, nor the place where the troops are stationed, nor by the number of cannon or of slaughtered men, but by that intangible force called the spirit of the army, and he watched this force and guided it in as far as that was in his power" (898).

Regarding all men's actions as predestined, though most notably actions of those in command of others, Tolstoy affirms, "It is true that we are not conscious of our dependence, but by admitting our free will we arrive at absurdity, while admitting our dependence on the external world, on time, and on cause, we arrive at laws" (1315). Herein lies Tolstoy's dilemma: he attempts to prove by analogies from science (particularly from physics and mathematics) the existence of laws which govern men's actions; and yet his most sympathetic characters arrive at these laws not by the rational process of science but by intuition.

Although "Science does not admit the conception of the ancients as to the direct participation of the Deity in human affairs" (1315), Tolstoy ultimately attributes to a Deity, the first cause, the cause of all the infinitely small causes which "move" history. In a lengthy description of an episode in the battle of Borodino the author traces the "one cause of all causes" to the "will of Him who governs men and worlds."

> *Over the whole field, previously so gaily beautiful with the glitter of bayonets and cloudlets of smoke in the morning sun, there now spread a mist of damp and smoke and a strange acid smell of saltpeter and blood. Clouds gathered and drops of rain began to fall on the dead and wounded, on the frightened, exhausted, and hesitating men, as if to say "Enough, men! Enough! Cease . . . bethink yourselves! What are you doing?"*

To the men of both sides alike, worn out by want of food and rest, it began equally to appear doubtful whether they should continue to slaughter one another; all the faces expressed hesitation, and the question arose in every soul: "For what, for whom, must I kill and be killed? . . . You may go and kill whom you please, but I don't want to do so any more!" By evening this thought had ripened in every soul. At any moment these men might have been seized with horror at what they were doing and might have thrown up everything and run away anywhere.

But though toward the end of the battle the men felt all the horror of what they were doing, though they would have been glad to leave off, some incomprehensible, mysterious power continued to control them, and they still brought up the charges, loaded, aimed, and applied the match, though only one artilleryman survived out of every three, and though they stumbled and panted with fatigue, perspiring and stained with blood and powder. The cannon balls flew just as swiftly and cruelly from both sides, crushing human bodies, and that terrible work which was not done by the will of a man but at the will of Him who governs men and worlds continued. (912–913)[33]

In this powerful description Tolstoy ascribes the "first cause" to the Deity, who is final arbiter of men's actions, prime mover of history, and the force which destroys the good and the bad indiscriminately. In the delineation of an amoral Deity Tolstoy returns "Him who governs men and worlds" to the status of Zeus not yet released from pre-Homeric tradition. Nevertheless, if Tolstoy has stressed too strongly the lack of freedom of will, ultimately, like Homer, he reveals that if man is not the master of his fate, he is in some sense an unconscious co-worker in shaping it.

Eventually the author, like Pierre, after focusing his mental telescope to see into remote space, throws away the telescope through which he has gazed over men's heads and is then able to focus his eyes on the unfathomable and infinite life around him (1227). Like Pierre and like others of his most remarkable characters, Tolstoy at length rejected scientific analogies as insufficient to explain the ineluctable. Only then was he able to recognize the ultimate inadequacy of the intellect to plumb the mystery of experience. As artist rather than philosopher, he abandoned mathematics for metaphor, reason for intuition, and philosophy for myth.

THE MYTHICAL PEASANT

According to Isaiah Berlin, Tolstoy sought a single, all-embracing standard throughout his life.[34] In the early part of *War and Peace* the standard is that of the good man, exemplified by most of his characters, notably Prince Andrew, Pierre, and General Kutuzov. Later in the epic, the standard is that of the peasant, who represents a simple Christian ethic divorced from abstruse principles of theology or metaphysics. Planton Karataev is the example. Tolstoy tells us that Karataev did not like talking about his life as a soldier, though he never complained. "When he related anything it was generally some old and evidently precious memory of his 'Christian' life, as he called his peasant existence." (1077–1078).[35]

We recall that the final conception of Karataev developed gradually. In the early drafts Tolstoy describes an old man, personifying the calm renunciation of earthly life. In one version the author inserts proverbs, mainly in narrative form; they do not yet come from the lips of Karataev.[36] Later the wisdom of age is uttered by Karataev, as in the incident of the Frenchman's linen shirt. Platon is described at work; then, producing the finished shirt he comments, "A promise is own brother of performance!" (1121). The Frenchman then asks for the scraps of linen which Karataev had hoped to keep for leg bands. At first pretending not to understand, he at length presents the scraps, which the Frenchman promptly returns. The enemy's generosity provokes another of Planton's proverbs: "People said they were not Christians, but they too have souls. It's what the old folk used to say: 'A sweating hand's an open hand, a dry hand's close' " (1121–1122).

Significantly, the influence of Karataev later guides Pierre in the final stage of his quest for a philosophy of life. Similarly, Homer's old men, with their sententious wisdom, reflect an interest in shaping the minds of youth during their malleable years in the accepted standards of *arete*. Exempla, the wisdom of generations condensed in gnomic utterances, serve in both Homer and Tolstoy as means of instruction. Hence they are often inserted in the speech of an old man; in age reposes wisdom, garnered and stored for generations to come. Old Karataev is also wise Karataev, as are Homer's Priam, Nestor, and Phoenix.

Homer introduces Priam sitting with the elders on the wall of Troy observing the battle—too old to fight but wise enough to give counsel. "Those who now ceased from battle for old age, yet were they right good orators, like grasshoppers that in a forest sit upon a tree and utter their lily-like voice; even so sat the elders of the Trojans upon the tower" (III, 150–155). Homer describes Nestor as one who had seen three generations of men go to battle, and "whom most of all the elders Agamemnon honored" (II, 21). But most important to the guidance of Achilles is the old tutor Phoenix, who taught the hero from infancy to be both a speaker of words and a doer of deeds—paramount in both. Phoenix reminds the hero, "Yea, I reared thee to this greatness, thou godlike Achilles, with my heart's love . . ." (IX, 485–486). In the scene of the Embassy to Achilles, Phoenix, whose devotion the hero cannot question, refers to the authority of the κλέα ἀνδρῶν (IX, 522), the heroic lays which have been transmitted from time immemorial as examples for young men to follow. In recounting the deeds of the model hero Meleager, Phoenix holds before Achilles' eyes a shining example. Meleager, at first overcome by wrath, was at length persuaded to relent. Let Achilles do likewise. This scene gives ethical import to the entire poem. Achilles does not relent. Accordingly, he suffers the consequences.

It is easy to concede the didactic influence of Homer without fully appreciating its import. As in the *Iliad,* in the scene of the Embassy to Achilles, exempla are always inserted in the mouth of a respected advisor whose duty it is to exhort young men to action consonant with the mores of the time. Thus in the *Odyssey,* Athena, goddess of wisdom, urges the young son of Odysseus, Telemachus, to follow the example of Orestes who so recently revenged himself on Aegisthus and Clytemnestra for murdering his father (I, 298–302). An earlier reference by Zeus to the moral problem of retribution, citing the example of Aegisthus and Orestes (*Odyssey* I, 32–47), justifies Athena's behest. Unlike Achilles, the docile youth of the *Telemachia* heeds the counsel of the goddess who is disguised first as his father's friend Mentes and later as another old friend,

Mentor, who guides him not only on the journey by sea but also on the more hazardous quest for manhood. Telemachus is thus schooled for his divinely appointed mission.

As in Homer, the older generation in *War and Peace* serve as models for the young to follow. Like Homer's Nestor, old Prince Bolkonsky reminds his son that men were braver when he was a general in the time of Catherine the Great, during the leadership of the warrior Suvorov. To set an historical example for future generations, the Old Prince offers an award to one who writes a history of Suvorov's wars (113). With characteristic irony, Tolstoy suggests that the old Prince may have illusions about the glories of the past, for his son Andrew quips, "The past always seems good" (106).

Of Tolstoy's exempla, none is more important in the development of the author's philosophy than the story Karataev tells Pierre many times in the French prison camp, that of the merchant accused of killing another merchant and sent unjustly to prison (1178). The story, later developed under the title "God Sees the Truth but Waits," bears the Russian title, "God Sees the Truth but Speaks Not Soon."[37] The anecdote invites careful examination because it exemplifies ideals toward which Tolstoy had been striving the greater part of his life. It is important in the Tolstoyan canon since the theme, that of forgiveness of wrongs, is the crux of the author's Christian ethic. That it was a favorite of Tolstoy's is apparent when we recall that in *What Is Art?* he cited it as the salient example of works illustrating the dominant requirement of art, that of religious perception.

Karataev's exemplum as it appears in *War and Peace* is brief, but its import is unmistakable. One night when the convicts were gathered, with the old merchant among them, they began telling what each was suffering for and how each had sinned against God. The old man's turn to speak comes. "I, my dear brothers," said he, "am being punished for my own and other men's sins. But I have not killed anyone or taken anything that was not mine, but have only helped my poorer brothers" (1179). Among the listeners is the very man who has accused the old merchant unjustly. The accuser confesses and asks of the old man forgiveness. The old man replies, "God will forgive you, we are all sinners in His sight. I suffer for my own sins." Now Karataev's face brightens as he is about to tell the meaning of the tale. The authorities appeal to the Tsar to set the old man free, and after long delay the pardon arrives. The authorities begin looking for the old man, "but God had already forgiven him—he was dead!" (1179).

In the retold tale, in which the old merchant is given the name Aksyenov, the author introduces two dramatic episodes. In the first episode Aksyenov's wife, visiting her husband in prison, reveals her doubt of his innocence. After the visit the merchant, recalling that his wife too suspects him, says to himself, "Evidently none but God can know the truth, and He alone must be asked, and from Him alone can I expect mercy." Henceforth Aksyenov no longer petitions the authorities for redress but only prays to God.

In the second episode of the retold tale, Aksyenov, during the twenty-six years of hard labor in Siberia, has opportunity to get revenge when he encounters among the new prisoners the very man who has accused him. One night after the prisoners have assembled, each relates the reason for his imprisonment. In the group is the very man responsible for Aksyenov's suffering. Realizing Makar is the culprit, Aksyenov is filled with wrath and desire for revenge. Later the opportunity presents itself when he detects Makar digging a hole to escape. But instead of revealing his knowledge to the authorities, Aksyenov remains silent before his inquisitors. The following night Makar falls down at Aksyenov's feet, confesses, and asks forgiveness: "You pitied me and did not tell on me. Forgive me, for Christ's sake!" he begs. Aksyenov answers, "God will forgive you. Maybe I am a hundred times worse than you!"

As in the exemplum related by Karataev, the retold tale ends with Aksyenov's death, but in the second version the old merchant's suffering appears less as a form of unjust punishment than as an act of beatification. Through his own anguish Aksyenov has learned to reconcile himself to his misfortune. We see clearly the key to the reconciliation in the moral the story teaches, that no man is untouched by sin and guilt and that only those who forgive can in turn be forgiven. Aksyenov enters fully into forgiveness through the knowledge of the common guilt of mankind, through recognition of the fact that each is responsible for the sins of all.

Aksyenov, who had confronted the problem of justice not only in himself but also in the world, acknowledges the omnipotence of God and his own dependence upon Him, even though he cannot hope to understand infinite wisdom. His acceptance is a final admission of his own finite limitations and a recognition of the inability of man to understand beyond the drastic limitations of human reason. In the end, Aksyenov's triumphant faith in God convinces him that man is not God's equal, and however sinless a man may feel himself to be, he cannot disannul God's judgment in order to justify himself.

In this regard a comment by Dostoevsky in the "Russian View of Guilt and Crime"is instructive. Dostoevsky explains: "He [God] alone knows the *whole* mystery of the world and man's ultimate destiny. And man, as yet, with the pride of infallibility, should not venture to solve anything—the times and the seasons have not yet come. The human judge himself must know that he is not the final judge; that he himself is a sinner; that in his hands—scales and measures will be an absurdity, *if* holding the scales and measures he fails to submit to the law of the still insoluble mystery and to resort to the only solution—to Mercy and Love."[38]

In forgiving an enemy, Aksyenov has acquitted himself and hence becomes entitled to acquittal at the hands of God. He has emulated the Deity in bestowing the blessings of mercy and love on his transgressor. As we have observed, the author expresses the doctrine of forgiveness in the mouths of a number of his leading characters: in the words of the dying Prince Andrew who forgives his personal enemy Anatole, and again in General Kutuzov's farewell address to his troops, as he forgives the national enemy, the French. But the most notable example appears in the person of the poor, uneducated peasant, Karataev, who epitomizes the highest Christian principles, culminating in submission of his will to that of the Divine: "Things happen not as we plan but as God judges" (1074).

In Tolstoy's ethic, forgiveness is inseparably linked with the doctrine of love. Observing the principle of forgiveness in the *Iliad*, Tolstoy was puzzled. Birukoff tells us that Tolstoy at twenty-nine, after reading the Gospels and the

Iliad, was moved by the beauty of both works. "I have finished reading the inexpressibly beautiful conclusion of the *Iliad*," he declared, and mentally comparing the two works, he regretted that there was no connection between them. "How could Homer fail to know that the only good is love?" he asked.[39]

Let us recall the conclusion of the *Iliad*. The old Trojan king, Priam, has come to Achilles' hut to redeem the body of his son Hector. Priam clasps in supplication the knees of Achilles and kisses his hands, "terrible, manslaying, that slew many of Priam's sons" (XXIV, 478–479). Priam entreats Achilles, "Have compassion on me, even me, bethinking thee of thy father. Lo, I am yet more piteous than he, and have braved what none other man on earth hath braved before, to stretch forth my hand toward the face of the slayer of my sons" (XXIV, 303–306). In compassion born of human suffering, each weeps for his own sorrow. Then Achilles, observing the rites of hospitality, invites Priam to satisfy his desire for meat and drink. That done, the two "enemies" look at each other, face to face, for the first time. Thereupon Priam marvelled at Achilles, "to see how great he was and how goodly, for he was like a god to look upon" (XXIV, 629–630). And Achilles, in turn, marvelled at Priam, "beholding his noble aspect and hearkening to his words" (XXIV, 631–632). Remembering that Priam too was happy once, Achilles returns the body unblemished. Two former enemies have "forgiven" each other.

At this point a comment by Frye is relevant: "It is hardly possible to overestimate the importance to Western literature of the *Iliad's* demonstration that the fall of an enemy, no less than of a friend or leader, is tragic and not comic. With the *Iliad*, once for all, an objective and disinterested element enters into the poet's vision of human life."[40] Homer's example of "forgiveness" seems the more remarkable when we reflect that in many parts of the world a feeling of forgiveness toward the enemy is regarded as contemptible.

In the episode of the ransoming of Hector, Homer demonstrates that he who, like Achilles, projects himself into the position of an antagonist has prepared himself to observe the enemy from an impersonal standpoint. Then it is that pity, which had at first extended only to himself, may unfold until it embraces not only the individual, his family, and his country, but finally all mankind. The custom of showing pity to one's fellowmen thus becomes an ethical principle.

Once we have discovered the custom among Homer's heroes, we may expect to find it also among the gods. Priam, in appealing to Achilles for pity (*eleos*), invokes the fear (*aidos*) of the gods who sanction *aidos*: "Yea, fear thou the gods, Achilles, and have compassion on me . . ." (XXIV, 503).[41]

If we grant that the existence of a custom among the gods constitutes infallible evidence of the age of a custom, we can hardly fail to be impressed by Homeric ethos at this early date. Though Zeus is frequently regarded as an amoral deity in Homer, the "father of gods and men" is here represented as taking pity on mankind. It is Zeus who is responsible for the reconciliation of Priam and Achilles. Zeus sent Achilles' mother to mollify her son, who had "cast out pity" (XXIV, 44), and bid him return the body of Hector. Zeus dispatched Iris to bid Priam go to Achilles' hut to ransom the body of Hector, and it was Zeus who sent

Hermes to attend Priam and thus secure safe passage through the lines of the enemy. Although Homer expounds no systematic theology, it is evident here that his ethics is nobler than his theology. While the gods in the *Iliad* are generally little concerned with questions of right and wrong, we must remember that these are primarily the gods of popular lore who retain characteristics with which they were endowed by poets of a primordial past.

The reception given Priam by Achilles, though it may be a late emendation, reveals a Zeus who exemplifies an ethical principle uncommon to epics of this early age, in fact uncommon in any age. It suggests that the Homeric Greeks had reached a stage of moral development in which they could treat with equality even an enemy; for when an impartial attitude is attributed to a god, it must first have appeared among men, since gods are, as Xenophanes reminds us, but magnified reflections of the men who worship them.[42]

Most epic heroes disdain those whom they oppose in war. For such antipathy there is sometimes a religious reason.[43] A familiar example is the *Chanson de Roland,* which demonstrates the superiority of Christendom over Islam.

Though in Homer's time the doctrine of loving an enemy had not yet been promulgated, the Homeric Greek seems to have been in touch with a principle as old as mankind, the apprehension that beyond the brotherhood of man there exists the great moral law that all men, because they are men, have equal worth in the sight of a universal God. Homer, however, limits his compassion with the proviso that his men—in order to be "men"—must be noble, possessed of the highest *arete.* Hence in Homer's ideal

97

world, of which a compassionate Zeus is exemplar, both Priam and Achilles—Trojan and Achaean—are godlike.

The source of Tolstoy's apprehension has been traced to the Sermon on the Mount (chapters five, six, and seven of St. Matthew's Gospel), which left an immense impression on the author before he was twenty-one. "From this Gospel code all of Tolstoy's principles are logically derived," Wiener tells us. "The injunction of loving our neighbor as ourselves in its ultimate application leads to the equality of all men."[44] Tolstoy, rightly called by Isaiah Berlin the "apostle of the gospel that all men are brothers," creates a democracy of Christendom in which both prince and peasant are equal. The common man ranks with the nobleman, since Christianity places no more value on the nobleman's soul than on the peasant's.

Tolstoy's insistence on the equality of men anticipates his views held more firmly in later life. Tolstoy had always felt great sympathy for the peasants who lived around him. He noted that they bore their hard lot patiently and when death came accepted it with tranquility. As Karataev taught Pierre to live in a relationship of love with all things, animate and inanimate, and that human existence has meaning only as man feels himself part of a whole, so Tolstoy in his association with the peasants evolved a philosophy of life based not on reason but on simple human feeling. By example as well as by words the peasant taught Tolstoy that God is everywhere.

About 1880, after what critics are disposed to call his "conversion," his mode of life changed. Dressed in his customary muzhik's smock, he now ate the peasant's fare and labored in the field with his peasants. In short, he began to enact the role he had praised in *War and Peace*.

Having reviewed his past, as told in the *Confession,* and having found much of it wanting, he turned his back on that which his own class held dear and began to practice more ardently the Gospel precepts he insisted were exemplified by the peasants.

That Tolstoy's enthusiasm for emulating the peasants had carried him to excess, Chekhov affirmed. Chekhov, grandson of a serf, and a man greatly admired by Tolstoy, observed: "War is evil and law is evil, but it does not follow from that that I must wear wooden shoes and sleep on the stove with my laborer and his wife. . . ."[45] With this view Count Tolstoy's wife agreed.

Metaphor

Chapter IV

METAPHOR,
THE LANGUAGE OF MYTH

S INCE to the Greeks all things had their excellence
(*arete*), animate and inanimate alike, we may speak of
virtues (ἀρεταί) of style. The style of epic poetry is
dignified by its figures of speech. We turn now from
thematic considerations (myth) to structural principles
(metaphor). A type of metaphor, the simile, is a common
figure of speech in epic poetry and it is the most common
figurative technique in *War and Peace*. Homer used similes
because of the exigencies of oral tradition. Virgil used
similes in the *Aeneid* because he was following Homer
(though Virgil is writing an art or literary epic in contrast to
Homer's popular or folk epic). Why does Tolstoy use
similes?

The question to be asked is why, in a literary derivation
of oral epic designed for a reading public rather than an
unlettered audience, similes should appear at all. Is Tolstoy
following tradition, though writing a prose epic?

The answer seems to lie in Frye's insistence upon the
tendency of great literature to resort to the primitive
exploitation of formulae. Frye emphasizes the indebtedness of great literature to an ancient heritage when he
insists that the "relation of later literature to these primitive
formulae is by no means purely one of complication, as we
find the primitive formulae reappearing in the greatest
classics—in fact there seems to be a general tendency on
the part of great classics to revert to them."[1]

While it has long been observed that Homer employs
certain conventions of epic poetry, notably the epithet and

103

the simile, it remained for Milman Parry to relate those conventions to the formulae which prevail in oral epic tradition. Parry tracked down the marks of ancient tradition in his exploration of oral epic among the Slavs of southern Europe in the early twenties of our century. There he observed singers reciting poems of great length through the use of formulae. His study of living epic tradition is of great service to the Homerist since it explains the way in which the epic singer composes and transmits his songs. Copious formulae are devised to assist the singer in the task of oral composition. Even when writing exists, the singer does not use it, for his is the art of improvising, not memorizing, though his recollection is aided by a large number of formulaic phrases.

In order to rebuild the formulaic structure of epic poetry, Parry demonstrated that Homer's epics are composed in a traditional style and that they are composed orally. He learned that the formula is the basis of Homeric style and that the use of formulae is governed by consistent rules which, in turn, are governed by the meter of epic versification—dactylic hexameter.

The oral poet does not work like the literary poet, who searches for the exact word, *le mot juste,* to impart originality to his style. When the oral poet unlocks his word-horde he follows his predecessors in the abundant use of formulae. Parry explains the intent of the oral poet: "Those who have sought to record oral poetry in lands where it still lives have straightway found that the same poem, that is to say, a poem on the same subject, could be sung badly or well, and that the people carefully set apart the poor singers from the good. Still the fame of such a singer comes not from quitting the tradition but from putting it to the best use. The poorer singer will repeat a poem with the loss of its most pleasing lines or its most dramatic moments, but the good singer will keep what is striking, and even add, on the pattern of other poems, lines which he knows will please, and new incidents, or give a fuller tale with many such borrowings. He may even have heard the same tale told by a singer living at a distance who inherited from a different tradition; then he will fuse the poems, using the best in each. Thus the highest sort of oral verse-making achieves the new by the best and most varied and perhaps the fullest use of the old."[2]

Homeric proverbs are examples of pleasing lines frequently borrowed by epic singers. In Homer, gnostic utterances crowd the memory, but two examples will suffice. In the first instance Nestor is advising Patroclus to urge Achilles to return to battle for

ἀγαθὴ δὲ παραίφασίς ἐστιν ἑταίρου.
"good is the persuasion of a friend." (XI, 793)

The identical formula is repeated when Patroclus says he must try to persuade Achilles to help his embattled countrymen (XV, 404).

In the second instance Menelaus is standing over the corpse of Patroclus and advising Euphorbus, who dealt the final blow, to desist lest he be slain for

ῥεχθὲν δέ τε νήπιος ἔγνω.
"by the event is even a fool made wise." (XVII, 32)

Euphorbus does not desist and is slain. The identical formula is repeated when Achilles, reminding Aeneas of his earlier escape from death, urges him to desist. Aeneas takes the advice and is saved (XX, 198).

We are reminded that Eliot acclaims the poet's novelty not in his differences from his predecessors but in resemblances when he says, "We shall often find that not only the best, but the most individual parts of his work may be those in which the dead poets, his ancestors, assert their immortality most vigorously."

The living poet's indebtedness to the dead poet is very clearly manifest in the use the living poet makes of the traditional epithet. Although in the use of the traditional epithet the living poet might recreate the old in a novel formulaic phrase, he consistently follows rules determined by meter and syntax, that is, by the demands of the hexameter and the inflectional system of Greek grammar.

Study of the Homeric epithet led Parry to the conviction that Homer followed the practice of earlier poets who sought the best and the easiest way of telling the same kind of stories in the same verse forms. Parry explains: "In my study of the traditional epithet in Homer I dealt with those formulas in the *Iliad* and in the *Odyssey* which are made up of a noun and one or more fixed epithets, and showed that they were created to help the poet set the heroic tale to hexameters. The noun has a metrical value which allows little change, but by adding to it an ornamental epithet one can make a phrase of the needed length which, since the epithet has no bearing on the idea of the sentence, can be used as freely as the simple noun. I also showed that the technique of the use of the noun-epithet formula is worked out to so fine a point that it could be only for the smallest part due to any one man."[3]

Bowra finds fifty-six different noun-adjective combinations for Achilles, for each is determined by the case of the noun and the position it occupies in the verse.[4] Sometimes the epithet is inappropriate, but often it is apt. For example, though Homer often refers to Achilles as fleet-footed, πόδας ὠκὺς Ἀχιλλεύς, the Achilles who prepares the funeral games for Patroclus is great-hearted, μεγάθυμος Ἀχιλλεύς. To take another apt illustration, Homer refers fifty times to the light in the eyes of the Goddess of Wisdom. She is "gleaming-eyed" goddess Athena, in the recurring epithet θεὰ γλαυκῶπις Ἀθήνη. Tolstoy, too, refers to the light in the eyes of one of his principal characters. Princess Mary's "luminous eyes" (1269 and elsewhere) are a distinguishing attribute.

We are now prepared to note the difference between the use of the epithet in poetic and in prose epic. In Homer the phrase appears in the last half of each verse, after the trochaic caesura of the third foot,[5] to fulfill the requirement of the meter. Like many of Homer's epithets, the phrase has been fossilized, but its use is imposed by epic convention. Tolstoy, on the other hand, has no need to conform to the strictures of meter; he has inherited no traditional epithets to aid in setting a heroic tale to hexameter.

Yet even the casual reader observes descriptive terms repeated in *War and Peace* with reference to certain characters. Tolstoy's purpose, as R. F. Christian observes, is to evoke in the reader a favorable or unfavorable response to his characters. Of Princess Mary, whose "soul always strove toward the infinite, the eternal, and the absolute, and could therefore never be at peace" (1305), Tolstoy approves. She is created in the author's own image, Maude tells us, "What Tolstoy here says of Countess [now the wife of Count Nicholas Rostov] Mary was very true of himself, and is an explanation of some of the aims and endeavors that have perplexed some readers of his later works."[6]

Christian distinguishes between the use of the epithet in classical epics and the stylistic use of a repeated description in Tolstoy.

Another variety of repetition and one which is characteristically Tolstoyan, is the constant reiteration of some external detail designed to characterize an individual: a repetition which has nothing to do with the fact that the novel is long and the reader's memory is short. No one can fail to notice how the essence of a Tolstoyan character is distilled into a mannerism, a gesture, a physical feature, an outward and visible sign which recurs continually and is the permanent property of that character. Such attributes are not repeated to remind us of something we have forgotten. Nor are they generalizations like the epithets pius *or* πολύμητις, *which qualify Aeneas and Odysseus, whether or not their behavior happens to be dutiful or resourceful. They represent rather musical* leit-motivs. *They identify the person by something more meaningful than a name and something less ossified than a stock epithet. The repeated reference to Napoleon's small white hands, Helene's bare white shoulders, Princess Marya's radiant eyes is not a conscious epic device. It is a combination of the assertion of a permanent, individualizing feature with the expression of a moral judgment. As well as suggesting what is most significant about his heroes, Tolstoy tries to evoke in the reader at the same time a positive or negative response to them. Napoleon's small hands suggest effeminacy and the absence of work. Helene's inadequate clothing is a sign of her brazenness; the light in Princess Marya's eyes reflects the inner light within her soul. We are intended to disapprove of Helene and Napoleon, and to approve of Princess Marya. This type of repetition of external detail, involving as it does the frequent recurrence of identical words, is an example of how closely related a novelist's language and characterization are.*[7]

When we understand that Homer's epithets relate to oral rather than written tradition, we cease to be puzzled by much that we find in Homer, and when we understand that Tolstoy's stylistic attributes relate to Christian tradition, we cease to be perplexed by much that we find in Tolstoy.

It is a common observation that Homer exalts everything he touches. Indeed, there is nothing which is not in some sense exalted if it partakes of the heroic tradition. Frequently even unsung heroes trail after them clouds of glory. When a minor hero appears in the *Iliad,* often as a victim of a major hero, Homer may grant him a memorial of a few lines in the manner of a panegyric. Thus Homer praises Iphidamas and Axylos. Iphidamas fell far from his wedded wife, his bride, "of whom he had known no joy," although for her he had given herds of cattle and had promised flocks of sheep and goats (XI, 242–243). Axylos was "dear to his fellows; for his dwelling was by the roadside and he entertained all men" (VI, 14–15).

Moreover, Homer animates everything he touches, he awakens it to life. Indeed, the animation seems to be the result of the exaltation. Aristotle gives examples, almost all from Homer, of metaphors that possess a lifelike quality, ἐνέργεια. [8] Memorable in the *Iliad* is the comparison of the heavy, helmeted head of a dying warrior to the head of a drooping poppy: "Even as in a garden a poppy droopeth its head aside, being heavy with fruit and the showers of spring; so bowed he aside his head laden with his helm" (VIII, 306–308).

In representing an experience Homer seems to have fulfilled the Apocalyptic promise, "Behold, I make all things new." And if we are to follow Victor Shklovsky's theory of "bestrangement," *ostranenie*, we perceive that Tolstoy too, by metaphorical comparison, is accustomed to make all things new and strange. According to Shklovsky, men normally develop a habitual response to experience, actual and artistic. As a given stimulus is repeated, a man ceases to perceive it and merely recognizes it. For instance, at the Council of War, Kutuzov, not listening to the monotonous voice reading dispositions for an attack, falls asleep. Then comes the bestranging simile, "When the monotonous sound of Weyrother's voice ceased, Kutuzov opened his eye as a miller wakes up when the soporific drone of the mill wheel is interrupted" (281). Perception can be awakened only by altering the stimulus, making it strange again. In Shklovsky's view, the purpose of art is to destroy automatic responses and to spark a new perception by altering the expected artistic pattern. Thus art, instead of reproducing, distorts the image of the world.[9]

As we have observed, one of the chief means of distorting an image, making it new and strange, is the use of simile. While an essential characteristic of the epithet is repetition, an essential characteristic of the simile is uniqueness. If we revert once more to the ubiquitous authority of Aristotle, we find that the simile is a kind of metaphor with a particle of comparison prefixed. Moreover, "The simile is also useful in prose, but should be less frequently used, for there is something poetical about it."[10]

What Aristotle says of the simile applies in large part to the metaphor. In the highest ranks of literary artists Aristotle places the creator of metaphor. To excel in the use of other aspects of style is admirable, "But the greatest thing by far is to have a command of metaphor. This alone cannot be imparted by another; it is the mark of genius, for to make good metaphors implies an eye for resemblances."[11] Proust, master of metaphor, believed that the metaphor gives a kind of eternity to style: *"Je crois que la metaphore seul peur donner une sorts d'eternite au style."* Let us examine a few epic similes, close cousin of the metaphor, before considering, in the next chapter, the more subtle implications of metaphor.

To consider all similes in the *Iliad* and in *War and Peace* would transcend the limits of this study.[12] Therefore we must confine ourselves to a small selection of representative examples taken from various areas of experience.

Comparison of anthropomorphic gods to animals is characteristic of a timeless tradition. We need but recall Homer's numerous types of animals sacred to various deities in ritualistic sacrifice. With mortals certain animals are also associated. To an ancient formulaic tradition Homer seems to be indebted when he describes Agamemnon surveying his forces "like a ram" and Hector rushing "like an eagle" on a flock of winged fowl, or when he so frequently describes warriors doing battle "like lions" or "wild boars."

Tolstoy's similes reveal a like interest in the animal kingdom: in horses, hounds, cattle, rams, hares, birds, bees, ants, and flies. The retreating French army, following its desolate route as it pursues its fatal course to Smolensk, is repeatedly likened to a mortally "wounded animal" (920, 1099, 1118, 1135, 1141). The looting French army, departing from pillaged Moscow, is compared to a monkey that has seized a handful of nuts in a jug with neck too narrow to allow the paw release; thus clinging to the nuts, the monkey, unwilling to abandon his loot, perishes.

Though Homer uses similes because they existed by virtue of the formulaic tradition, he seems in some instances to be drawing upon his own repertory of vivid phrases to ornament a conventional image, and thus to make his own contribution to the heroic tradition. It is not easy to differentiate the traditional from the original, though that which is original with the author seems to expand to capture the emotional associations of the poet's world. Original ornamentation, as well as conventional repetition, thus becomes traditional usage. Let us illustrate. Twice Homer compares a man going to battle with a stallion going to pasture. Paris goes to war as he goes to love, like a stallion (VI, 506–511), and Hector goes to battle like an eager stallion (XI, 548–554). In addition to the image of the stallion, we note the vivid ornamentation. Similes such as these seem to "illustrate the heroic past in terms of the known present."[13]

Let us take another example. The comparison of the stars in the moonlit midnight sky to watchfires of the Trojans encamped on the plain, as they anticipate the destruction of the Achaeans at dawn (VIII, 555–565) is famous. Then the poet tells us in a remark seemingly irrelevant, but entirely characteristic of the ornamental simile, that seeing the peaceful heavens "the shepherd's heart is glad." In more homely imagery, Tolstoy describes in metaphor the celestial bodies as they appear to soldiers sitting around campfires ("the soldiers' kitchens" [857]). "Look at the stars. It's wonderful how they shine! You might think the women had spread out their linen," says a soldier gazing in admiration at the Milky Way (1215).

112

Not without purpose both Homer and Tolstoy interpose amid scenes of war scenes of peace, filled with imagery designed to relieve emotional tension. The long simile, like a scene of comic relief in a tragedy, invites us for the moment to forget the excitement, or even the monotony of war, which otherwise might overwhelm us and dull our sensibilities. We afterwards return to the battle with regained interest.

Not without design Homer uses in the *Iliad*, against the background of war, four times as many similes as in the *Odyssey*, and not surprising is the observation that in the *Iliad* 164 similes appear in scenes of war while but thirty-eight appear in scenes of peace.[14]

Though Homer's similes are frequently long, never does one reach the length of Tolstoy's simile of the bees, which expands to cover almost two pages. Moscow, half deserted before the entrance of Napoleon, is compared to a dying queenless hive which has lost leadership. Of this lengthy simile Christian observes: "It is quite possible that the complex extended simile such as the one comparing deserted Moscow to a queenless hive is a conscious imitation of an epic device, a prose counterpart of the bees similes in the *Georgics* or in *Paradise Lost*," or in the *Iliad*.[15]

Between the epics of Homer and Tolstoy there exists yet another likeness in the use of clusters of similes to mark a climax. Whether by design or by coincidence, at a crucial point in *War and Peace* Tolstoy, like Homer in the *Iliad*, piles four similes. In the *Iliad* the flight of Hector before he stands to face Achilles is expressed by images of a dove fleeing before a falcon, charioteers competing in a race, a fawn fleeing before a hound, and two dreamers—one in flight, the other in pursuit (XXII, 139–201). In *War*

113

and Peace four similes, though more mundane than those in the *Iliad,* describe the exodus of the French army from Moscow. The French army disperses uncontrollably like a hungry herd of cattle or like water percolating through sand, with the result described in two additional similes, that both Moscow and the army are destroyed, as when water is spilled on dry ground and disappears or as sparks ignite a heap of shavings (999).

More pretentious are Tolstoy's scientific images, found mainly in the author's exposition of his philosophy of history. Drawn for the most part from the physical world of mass and momentum, these images reveal the interest of a cultured layman with a capacity to interpret imaginatively the achievements of science. Though they are seldom commonplace, they are never recondite.

In the sphere of art Tolstoy had wider acquaintance, as extensive observations in *What Is Art?* indicate. An art which held a strong fascination for him was the theater, if we are to judge by the number of images taken from the theatrical sphere. Memorable is the episode of Natasha's view of the opera in Moscow (620–624). In the extended theatrical metaphor Natasha is newly awakened to an artificial world, not only on the stage but also in the audience. Like Shakespeare, Tolstoy reminds us frequently that all the world's a stage, and metaphor is the universal language.[16]

THE METAPHORICAL CIRCLE

Greek Anthropocentric View

The circle is universally accepted as a symbol of eternity. The significance of the circle and the sphere, associated with the manifestation of the divine in nature, has haunted the imagination of men for ages.

A glance at the circular motif reveals its import in pagan iconography. In the *Iliad* the "sacred circle" is represented by Achilles' shield, where around the rim flows the ocean embracing the world of Homeric civilization, one city at war, the other at peace. In the city at peace, elders are sitting in a sacred circle ready to adjudicate a quarrel between two men concerning the blood-price to be paid for a man who has been slain. To the early Greek the sanctity of the circle was expressed by the orchestra, the circular dancing place for worshipers celebrating the ritual around the altar of the god of wine, Dionysus, in whose honor tragedy traditionally originated.

To the author of comedy—if we can trust the brilliant discourse assigned by Plato to Aristophanes in the *Symposium*—we are indebted for the explanation of Love by attributing the origin to primeval cosmic circle-men. Aristophanes' speech begins as a *jeu d'esprit*, a fantasy describing the first human beings, who rebelled against the gods and were bisected in punishment for their pride. Each human being was originally a whole with back and flanks rounded to form a circle. Each had four hands, four legs, and two identical faces upon a circular neck, with one head common to both faces, which were turned in opposite directions. Each had four ears and everything else to correspond. These beings could walk upright in every direction, backwards or forwards, but when they wanted to run rapidly they used all eight legs, and turned over and over in a circle, like a tumbler who performs a cartwheel and returns to an upright position.

They were akin to circular celestial bodies. Originally the male sprang from the sun and the female from the earth, while the sex which was both male and female came from the moon, which partakes of the nature of both sun and earth. Both their spherical shape and their hoop-like method of progression were due to the fact that they were like their parents.

Contemporary beings, now bisected, Aristophanes explains, are merely halves of original wholes, which were of three sexes: male, female, and androgyne, but each individual attempts to regain his original happy state by uniting himself with his lost half, by coming together and throwing his arms about another—eager to grow into one. Love, concludes Aristophanes, is "the desire and pursuit of the whole."

The metamorphosis of the circle, from the time of Parmenides, Plato, Plotinus, Boethius and others bridges many centuries, until, as a result of the zealous teaching of the scholastics, the pagan circle acquired Christian overtones.

Christian Theocentric View

In Christian iconography, to mention but a few of many examples, the rose window of the cathedral symbolizes the wholeness of God. In El Greco's famous painting, the "Burial of Count Orgaz," the artist's son points to the encircled white and gold rose embroidered on St. Stephen's vestment—the circle as the symbol of immortality and the rose of love. The circle is identified also with the serpent biting his tail (ouroboros), exemplifying a living creature whose end is joined to the beginning; for did not

116

Christ affirm that He is both beginning and end, the alpha and omega of existence, the end of earthly life and the beginning of a heavenly one.

In Tolstoy's masterpiece the symbolic circle expresses philosophical precepts of more than one character. It appears, however, most patently in the representation of two seemingly disparate characters, Count Pierre Bezukhov and the peasant, Platon Karataev, who becomes the salient influence in the regeneration of Pierre.

Like many heroes engaged in a quest,[17] Pierre, before he encountered Karataev, had sought the meaning of life multifariously: in dissipation, in philanthropy, in freemasonry. As a curious neophyte, in freemasonry Pierre thought he had found promise of extraordinary enlightenment. He felt he was starting on the path of regeneration leading to a virtuous life (387). As the initiation ceremony begins Pierre is asked to surrender all valuables he has with him, including his watch, his rings, his money, all round objects offered "in token of generosity" (390). Eventually as a "Seeker," a "Sufferer," and a "Postulant" he is ready to complete his pilgrimage among the round compasses and candles and other symbolic objects of the Masonic order.[18] Eventually he realizes the folly and futility of his quest.

Pierre's quest to understand war leads to an equally absurd position. Uninitiated by experience, Pierre appears as a casual observer in a white hat while he views the battlefield from a quiet knoll before he receives his baptism of fire (884). Here the circular pattern appears in the cannon balls, harbingers of death and grim reminders of eternity. In this example of "bestrangement" Pierre learns that war is not what he thinks it is. His education has begun.

When Pierre, taken captive, encounters Karataev in the French camp for prisoners of war, he is aware of the peasant's uncomplaining acceptance of the rigors of camp life. Bivouacking with other prisoners at the end of a march, Pierre hears Platon mutter his evening prayer, "Lay me down like a stone, O God, and raise me up like a loaf" (1076). The homely imagery of the stone and the loaf, both circular, carry deep natural overtones associated with the earth.

In another scene of bivouac after a march of the captives, Pierre regards the heavenly bodies philosophically, as the "limitless distance" lures him to itself. Glancing at the sky with its twinkling stars, Pierre reflects, "And all that is me, all this is within me, and it is all I!" (1130)[19] Pierre's apprehension of the *all* in nature embraces circular archetypal patterns, to mention but a few, of sun, moon, earth, the arc of the horizon, the pebbles rounded by the sea, the chalice of a flower, the bole of a tree, the nest of a bird, and the orbs of the eyes of the beholder.

From atom to universe, all are part of the Whole of nature such as Pierre had observed earlier, during the symbolic journey on the ferry. Expounding on the theme of eternity to his skeptical friend Andrew, Pierre there observes, "We must live, we must love, and we must believe that we live not only today on this scrap of earth, but have lived and shall live forever, there in the Whole" (422). Pointing to the sky, Pierre envisions the whole of nature as the content of an infinite and eternal living body represented by the symbol of the sphere.

Pierre's quest ends in his discovery of the simple Christian ethic embodied in the peasant Karataev, living in rapport with nature and accepting his misfortunes as blessings. Observing the elemental precepts and example of Karataev, "an unfathomable, rounded, eternal personification of the spirit of simplicity and truth" (1078), Pierre learns to accept life complacently. His regeneration has begun.

In the author's early drafts Pierre's regeneration was achieved without the influence of Karataev. Later in the drafts Pierre, retreating from the battlefield at Borodino, encounters an old man, who is described briefly as "the personification of old age—tranquility, renunciation of earthly life, equanimity." This is the first hint of Karataev. In a subsequent version he is introduced abruptly and the roundness theme is developed. Other versions follow, until in the final draft the author introduces Karataev through the effect he has on Pierre and the roundness theme is emphasized.[20] This theme needs a little more attention.

Upon first meeting Karataev, Pierre is aware of something well "rounded" in the circular movements of the prisoner's arms as he unwinds his leg bands, and later when in a sitting position he clasps his arms around his lifted knees (1073). The "round" motif continues. "When Pierre saw his neighbor next morning at dawn the first impression of him, as of something round, was fully confirmed. Platon's whole figure—in a French overcoat girdled with a cord, a soldier's cap, and bast shoes—was round. His head was quite round, his back, chest, shoulders, and even his arms, which he held as if ever ready to embrace something, were rounded, his pleasant smile and his large, gentle brown eyes were also round" (1076–1077). In the original Russian the word *krugly* (round) appears five times in one sentence. The author tells us that to Pierre, Platon "always remained what he had seemed that first night: an unfathomable, rounded, eternal personification of the spirit of simplicity and truth" (1078).

In a later episode the "round" motif again appears. Karataev is making a shirt for a tattered French soldier. He is described at work with the familiar repetition of the word "round." "His hair was bound round, workman fashion, with a wisp of limetree bast, and his face seemed rounder and pleasanter than ever" (1121). At length, having finished the shirt, with "one of his round smiles," he observed his handiwork.

Later, when the order to march is given, Platon, weak and ill with fever, looks at Pierre "with his kindly round eyes now filled with tears" (1180). He remains leaning against a birch tree when a shot rings out, and the blue-gray bandy-legged bitch, Karataev's constant companion, begins to howl.

Though Karataev dies on the march among the prisoners of war, the next night in a dream Pierre remembers the lesson Platon has taught him—"to love this life in one's sufferings, in innocent sufferings" (1181). Pierre's dream links the essence of the peasant soldier's teaching with the image of the constant flux of life in a God-centered universe. The motif of roundness in the form of a globe composed of fluid drops dominates Pierre's last vision of Karataev. In his dream a kindly old man who had given him geography lessons in Switzerland shows him a globe, a ball made of drops constantly moving—merging and dividing. "That is life," says the old teacher. . . . God is in the midst, and each drop tries to expand so as to reflect Him to the greatest extent. And it grows, merges, disappears from the surface, sinks to the depths, and again emerges. There now, Karataev has spread out and disappeared" (1181–1182).[21]

Karataev, the expanding drop, has merged and disappeared, but like the other drops he will come again. In the sphere, with God in the midst, Karataev's soul will reappear since death is not a final event but a sign of God's transcendence made immanent. Herein lies the paradox which locates the infinite in the finite. Pierre, in an epiphany, the perception of the divine in human form, now apprehends the mystery of the Whole, perpetuating itself in its creations everlastingly. Pierre has glimpsed eternity in a moment of vision.

We have observed the significance of the circle primarily as it relates to the regeneration of Pierre through the influence of Karataev. Let us look now at the last reference to the peasant, in the scene of domestic happiness which Pierre finds with Natasha and their four children. Here the relation between the child and the circle is paramount. We recall that Karataev had once inquired of Pierre, "Well, and have you little ones?" Receiving a negative answer, Platon had consoled himself by the thought that Pierre was still young. He found further consolation in a misfortune. As punishment for stealing wood in a copse he had been sent as a soldier in lieu of a brother who had "five little ones," while he left only a wife.

As Pierre and Natasha recall the childlike peasant, Pierre wonders whether Platon would be pleased with his way of life. Concerning his effort to become a *salvator mundi* (savior of the world), to give a new direction to the government by uniting honest people, Pierre is convinced

Karataev would have been apprehensive, but he is confident he would have approved of their family happiness (1307).

We recall an earlier passage in which Pierre discovered that Platon's face, "despite its fine, rounded wrinkles, had an expression of innocence and youth" (1077). The motif of the innocent child has wide implications. The image of the intuitive child, as it relates to Christian doctrine, is apparent in the prominence given the casual observer, the peasant child Malasha, at the crucial Council of War which is to decide the fate of Moscow. Malasha is sitting on the oven observing the animosity of the generals who contend for influence at the council meeting held in her father's cottage at Fili. Tolstoy describes the scene: "Malasha, who kept her eyes fixed on what was going on before her, understood the meaning of the council differently. It seemed to her that it was only a personal struggle between 'Grandad' [Kutuzov] and 'Long-coat' as she termed Bennigsen. She saw that they grew spiteful when they spoke to one another, and in her heart she sided with 'Grandad' " (927).

In contrast to the theocentric teachings of Tolstoy, whose child with intuitive wisdom stands near to the kingdom of Heaven, Homer's anthropocentric tradition gives the child no such exalted position. Homer's boy in the *Iliad* stands with his feet planted firmly on earth, though he "scatters the sand beside the sea, first making sand buildings for sport in his childishness, and then again, in his sport, confounding them with his feet and hands" (XV, 362–364).

In accord with his ideal of "simplicity, goodness, and truth" Tolstoy emphasizes that the views of a child, which have sprung from childlike intuition into the truth of experience, excel the logical perceptions of maturity. If this view is naive, it is also Christlike.

In the apotheosis of the Christlike peasant Karataev, Pierre's earlier conviction, expressed in the scene on the ferry, is confirmed, "We who are now the children of the earth are—eternally—children of the whole universe" (421). Creation is the work of a God who is reflected in the human sphere, which in turn tries to reflect him. Herein lies the paradox of the Incarnation, the Father manifest in the divine Child, who assumed a human form. The Christ child descended to the center of creation, into the round womb of the world.

Poets as well as philosophers and theologians have found fruitful the image of the child. The English poet Richard Crashaw in his "Epiphanie Hymn," entitled "In the Glorious Epiphanie of Our Lord God" (companion poem to his Nativity Hymn), reveals pagan kings from the East converging toward the central place where the Savior of the World was born. In chorus the kings who have come to worship the new Light sing:

> O, little all, in Thy embrace
> The world lies warm, and likes his place;
> Nor does his full globe fail to be
> Kiss'd on both his cheeks by Thee. (36–39)

In the poem the immensity of the world becomes a toy—a ball—in the hands of a child, while the smallness of the child becomes the immensity of a God who embraces the universe.

Another reference to the Child and the universe bears scrutiny. It is told that St. Christopher, proud of his great physical strength, was willing to serve only the strongest. First he served a king, but when he learned that the king feared the devil, he left and began to serve the devil. Then one day he discovered that the devil feared the crucifix, whereupon he decided to serve Christ if he could find Him. A priest advised him to wait for Christ at a ford. During the years of waiting he carried many persons across the river. Then, on a dark, stormy night a small child called out that he wanted to be carried across. With the greatest of ease St. Christopher lifted the child on his shoulders and set out. As he walked his burden became heavier with every step, so that when he arrived in midstream, he felt "as if he carried the whole universe." He realized then that he had taken Christ upon his shoulders, and Christ gave him remission of sins and eternal life.[22]

Taught by the childlike Christian peasant, Pierre at the conclusion of *War and Peace* has found, in the month's captivity during which time he ate baked potato and buckwheat soup with horseflesh, the tranquility for which he had been striving. Like Dante, in the circular symbols of state and church, he has been crowned and mitred over himself. When in humility he takes the symbolic universe on his back, even as did the patron saint of travelers, St. Christopher (bearer of Christ), his inward journey ends. Not irrelevant at this point is the double implication of the Russian word *mir,* meaning world or peace. In apprehension of the *mir,* the "little All," Pierre's quest has come full circle.

Chapter V

THE MYTH OF THE HERO: FROM WAR TO PEACE

THE MYTH of the hero had intrigued Tolstoy from the time of his early military service in the Caucasus. From that time until the end of his life his attitude toward heroism in war changed perceptibly, though even his early sketches, some of which were written on the battlefield, reflect a growing condemnation of warfare and a questioning of conventional heroism. Before tracing Tolstoy's emerging attitude toward war, let us glance at the Homeric background.

As Athena issued full-armed from the head of Zeus, so the Homeric hero seems to have sprung full-grown and full-armed from the old heroic lay which, in turn, traces its origin to myth. To the myth of the birth of a short-lived, semi-divine hero we are indebted for the creation of Achilles, while to Homer we are indebted for the development of the saga of the heroic Achilles as an epic archetype.

In the panoply of war was born the heroic code of Homeric epic which confirmed the Greeks in their exaltation of military exploits. Homer, however, does not accept the primitive code wholeheartedly. In Homeric epic every hero hungers after eternal glory. He insists upon receiving his "meed of honor," which he measures by his achievement of *arete*.

Later Greeks, Plato and Aristotle, condone war as essential to their mode of life. Aristophanes, on the other hand, saw clearly the cost of war to the individual. Aristophanes spoke boldly for peace and satirized the generals and politicians who lined their pockets during the Peloponnesian War.

Tolstoy's early emphasis directs us to the bravery of the common soldier, the man in the ranks who first shouts "Hurrah!" or "We are lost!" Upon him, according to the author, depends victory or defeat in battle. The common soldier, or sometimes a lesser officer, is frequently the hero of the war stories for which Tolstoy won his early reputation. Such men the author had encountered on the battlefield.

Twenty-two years old, dissatisfied with efforts to study literature and philosophy, to improve the lot of the peasants on his estate, and to curb his desire for women and cards, Tolstoy, in a spirit of adventure, joined his brother Nikolai, who was returning to his post in the Caucasus. A new life of action began for Tolstoy when, in June 1852, he was allowed to participate as a volunteer in a raid on a Chechen hill village. After the raid the general commended him for bravery and recommended he petition to enter the army. *The Raid,* published in *The Contemporary* in March 1853, is an account of his experience but, more significantly, it is a disputation on men's motives for shedding blood.

The first line of *The Raid* announces the narrator's attitude: "War has always fascinated me." Not, he explains, the movement of armies but "how a soldier kills and what makes him do it." The narrator inquiries, too, about courage, when accompanying a raiding party he finds disparate examples of "heroism" in action. On the one hand there is Captain Khlopov, the seasoned warrior, sitting bravely and wisely on his horse, calmly performing his duty. He has no illusions about war, he does not glorify military action; he knows that on every raid one or more of his comrades will be killed. In contrast, the young

126

officer Alanin, overcome by the desire to display courage in his first military encounter, disobeys the captain's orders and, brandishing his unsheathed saber high in the air, plunges daringly and foolishly into the forest, to return wounded and die. Like the narrator, Tolstoy is beginning to perceive that the romantic life he had envisioned in the Caucasus is less idyllic than he had anticipated. "And is it a display of courage when a man, out of sheer vanity, risks his own life in order to kill a fellow creature?" the narrator wonders.

In *Sevastopol in May* the question of courage, adumbrated in *The Raid*, reverberates. Tolstoy asks again, Why *do* men kill one another? The truth, he concludes, is not what men think it. In midst of superhuman courage there is vanity and the desire for an extra medal. Nor is death in battle always noble. Who, then, is the hero? Who the fool?

Tolstoy describes a scene reminiscent of Homer's *Iliad*. In the *Iliad* two enemies, Glaucus and Diomedes, meet on the battlefield. Finding that their grandfathers, as guest-friends, had entertained each other and given gifts, the two exchange armor and agree not to fight one another. Similarly in the Sevastopol sketch Tolstoy describes a moment of amity. When flags of truce are raised a Frenchman, crossing the barrier, gives a wooden cigar holder to a Russian as a memento of their meeting, and a Russian gives a like token in exchange. Who, then is the hero, who the villain?

The question of heroism recurs in *The Cossacks*, a story which occupied the author's attention intermittently for ten years. During that time he read the *Iliad* in translation twice.[1]

Since *The Cossacks* is generally recognized as the seminal work of the author's career, and the masterpiece of his early years, the story bears further scrutiny. Especially noteworthy are the autobiographical elements. Like the fictional Olenin, Nikolai and Leo Tolstoy spent the night in convivial farewell before they set out, in May 1851, on a trip down the Volga to Astrakhan and finally to the Cossack village where Nikolai's army detachment was stationed. Like Olenin, Tolstoy wished to enter into the strong, free, and beautiful life of his imagined men of nature, to start a new life free of Moscow diversions. His diary reveals he had limited success. Despite good intentions, the cadet in the Caucasus frequently reproaches himself for continued "sensuality" and "vanity" among the mountaineers.

In the Caucasus Tolstoy encountered models for two of his main characters, Epishka, the Eroshka of the tale, and Solomonide, the model for Maryanka. For the fictional Lukashka he needed no prototype. Tradition teems with such characters. Lukashka's prowess in war suggests the archetypal epic hero, although as a Cossack the young warrior emerges from the fabled Cossack world romantically depicted by Pushkin, Lermontov, and others.

The Cossacks, as Tolstoy describes them in Chapter IV, were descendants of a group of Old Believers—those who had separated from the Orthodox Church in the seventeenth century—and still proudly maintained their old traditions. The small Christian clan, surrounded by half-savage Mohammedan tribes and by Russian soldiers, "acknowledges none but Cossacks as human beings and despises everybody else." Having intermarried with their Tartar foe, however, they often hate less a Chechen who may have killed a brother than the Russian soldier quartered in the village for defence, but who remains an oppressor.

To this village comes Olenin, a jaded young Muscovite, escaping the society of the elite and an unhappy love affair. All unpleasant reminiscences vanish at the sight of the mountains. "And the mountains!" The refrain echoes Olenin's enchantment, ending with his complete absorption in the scene. "From the village comes a Tartar wagon, and women, beautiful young women, pass by . . . and the mountains! Abreks canter about the plain, and here am I driving along and do not fear them! I have a gun, and strength, and youth . . . and the mountains!" Among the untrammeled and warlike Cossacks Olenin feels he will be happy.

Here the male population of the village spend their time on military expeditions or "at their post." At the post Olenin encounters Lukashka, who has lately joined the Cossacks at the front. Lukashka has already acquired the calm assurance of a Cossack and the "somewhat proud and warlike bearing peculiar to Cossacks and to men generally who continually carry arms." Lukashka will soon prove that he can kill like a Cossack.

To Lukashka killing is a way of life. Whether to destroy bird, beast, or man, he exults in his unflinching "courage." In the light of highly critical views taken of killing in earlier stories, such as *The Raid* and the Sevastopol sketches, the author's denigration of youthful "heroism" becomes increasingly clearer. Lukashka is the focus of such judgment.

Although Lukashka is mentioned early in the story, when his mother insists that her son would be an admirable match for Maryanka, we first encounter him in the cordon, in Chapter VI, as he awaits an attack by the Tartars. Tolstoy prepares us for his display of "heroism" when a pheasant caught in his net is brought him by a friend, Nazarka.

> *"I don't like killing them," said Nazarka.*
> *"Give it here!"*
> *Lukashka drew a little knife from under his dagger and gave it a swift jerk. The bird fluttered, but before it could spread its wings the bleeding head bent and quivered.*
> *"That's how one should do it," said Lukasha, throwing down the pheasant. "It will make a fat pilau."*

Presently the author gives another example. As Lukashka is on the way to ambush on the river bank, a boar leaps out of the water and disappears among the reeds. "Lukashka pulled out his gun and aimed, but before he could fire the boar had disappeared in the thicket. Lukashka spat with vexation and went on."

Undaunted by killing of bird or beast, Lukashka is now ready to kill his first abrek (Tartar brave). "Supposing I killed an abrek all by myself!" he reflects. Presently he discerns an abrek, a scout swimming in the river, concealed under a floating log. Finding the gun sight, Lukashka blesses himself, "In the name of the Father and of the Son," and fires. The startling anomaly of blessing himself as he pulls the trigger never occurs to Lukashka. As he waits for the patrol to arrive from the cordon in order to recover the body, he is tormented by the thought that the other abreks might escape. "He was vexed with the abreks who were going to escape just as he had been with the boar that had escaped the evening before."

Although Tolstoy does not denigrate Lukashka's indomitable enthusiasm and virile energy, he emphasizes that these traits accompany a youthful vanity and moral callousness. Lukashka finds joy in killing itself. John Hagan, commenting on "Ambivalence in Tolstoy's *The Cossacks*," observes, "What is disturbing is not so much that Lukashka carries out his military duties with the unreflecting efficiency and discipline of one for whom warfare has become a completely accepted way of life, but that he so obviously relishes these duties. He has no more moral life than a bold and splendid animal."[2]

Lukashka, however, as a fictional character, Tolstoy was at liberty to describe as he pleased, but the ancient warrior Eroshka, modeled upon the Epishka of the Caucasus, displays similar ambivalent attributes, the ambivalence of Christian characteristics of the Old Believers blended with heathen characteristics adopted as a result of centuries of exposure to Tartar culture.

As *The Cossacks* was originally conceived, Eroshka, identified as Epishka in the diary of January 7, 1854, was to have a more significant role than that given the old hunter and boon companion of Lukashka in the published story. As the diary of October 18 and 21, 1852, indicates, the "amazing stories" told by Epishka were to be included in the "Caucasian Sketches."[3] Work on the sketches was interrupted by service in the Danubian army and at the siege of Sevastopol, although Tolstoy's interest in the life of the Caucasus and his sporadic recording of former experiences did not cease.

In the final work the amazing stories told by Eroshka reveal an incongruous blend of Christian and heathen attitudes, especially toward the practice of killing. Eroshka boasts of his youthful exploits, in which "the death of more than one Russian, as well as Chechen, lay on his conscience." In Lukashka's drinking, plundering, whoring, and killing he finds an epitome of his own youth.

Too old to fight, Eroshka spends most of his time hunting. Yet as a superannuated warrior, he voices concern on more than one occasion for the killing of both human and non-human creatures. A babe's cradle floating down the river suggests to Eroshka that a Russian soldier has invaded a Tartar village and killed the little one, "taken it by the legs, and hit its head against a wall." Of the death of a pig, "wiser than a man," he laments, "It is a pig, but it is no worse than you—it too is God's creature." And the moths circling around the candle flame invoke Eroshka's sympathy as he catches them tenderly with his thick fingers. "You are killing yourself and I am sorry for you!"

It may be argued that Eroshka is attempting to impress Olenin with his display of compassion, for his actions sometimes belie his words. Although he expresses reservations about Lukashka's joy in killing his first abrek, at the same time he exults in the youth's achievement. Upon hearing Lukashka carolling a merry song because he has killed a Chechen, Eroshka remarks to Olenin, "And what is there to rejoice at?" Though a seasoned killer, Eroshka insists, "It is a serious thing to destroy a human being." Nevertheless, as morning dawns, Eroshka, already in his cups, leaves Olenin for Lukashka's victory celebration, where he drinks a toast to the victor. "Your health! To the Father and the Son!" Then follows the prayer and praise, "May you have what you desire, may you always be a hero, and obtain a cross." As represented by Eroshka, the

Christianity originally practised has been reduced to a few empty gestures and phrases. Religion, in the belief of Eroshka, offers no sanction for morality, for "When you die the grass will grow on your grave and that's all."

Confronting this ambivalence in values, Olenin at first finds pleasure in the Cossacks' freedom from moral law. After hunting with Eroshka in the forest, though his booty, the stag and the pig, have escaped, Olenin returns tired, hungry, and happy. Eating and drinking with Eroshka, he views existence with the Cossacks ecstatically. Here are the mountains and Maryanka. "Again, to the west, the mountains rose before his eyes. Again the old man told his endless stories of hunting, of abreks, of sweethearts, and of all that free and reckless life. Again the fair Maryanka went in and out across the yard, her beautiful powerful form outlined by her smock."

The next day Olenin goes hunting alone in the forest. In the crucial scene, in Chapter XX, with seven pheasants tied around his belt, he comes to the lair of a stag in a thicket. As he lies down in the stag's lair a feeling of love overwhelms him and he begins crossing himself and thanking someone. The mosquitoes no longer plague him; they are individuals like himself. Indeed, he feels himself another mosquito, a pheasant, or a stag, like those around him. The mystery revealed to Olenin in this evanescent communion with nature, this epiphany, lies in the apprehension that "happiness consists in living for others." This episode Hagan regards as the turning point in the development of Olenin, for "A moral consciousness has been born in Olenin, and it will not let him rest."[4]

In this scene the benign world of nature echoes the moral order. As in *The Raid*, Tolstoy here endues

133

nature with power to guide men's actions. In the earlier work the author describes a march through the beautiful scenery of the Caucasian mountains: "Can it be that there is not room for all men on this beautiful earth under these immeasurable starry heavens? Can it be possible that, in the midst of this entrancing nature, feelings of hatred, vengeance, or the passion for exterminating their fellows can endure in the souls of men? All that is unkind in the hearts of men ought, one would think, to vanish at the touch of nature, that most direct expression of beauty and goodness."

But nature, like man, may be ambivalent. To Olenin who has lost his way in the forest the turbulence of a storm causes him to doubt his new-found convictions. Suddenly, however, the sun appears, lighting the scene of the ransoming of the body of the abrek slain by Lukashka.

This episode may be compared to the scene of the ransoming of the body of Hector in the final book of the *Iliad*. As Hector's body, stripped of armor, is preserved unblemished, so the abrek's corpse, stripped of weapons, is saved from the jackals. Like King Priam, the dead man's brother "calm and majestic as a king," comes to claim the body—though one is in royal robes, the other in rags. Here the likeness ends and the antithetical operation of the revenge motif begins. Whereas in the *Iliad* the desire for revenge ceases with the reconciliation of former foes, in *The Cossacks* the revenge motif commences with the urge for retribution from the enemy. Having paid the ransom money, the brother of the slain Chechen, after entering the skiff with the body, casts a look of "cold contempt" on the man pointed out as the slayer, Lukashka. The taciturn abrek's look of "cold contempt" as he ransoms his brother, Ahmet Khan, bodes ill for the "hero" Lukashka.

In the ransoming scene the authorial character, Olenin, perceives vaguely Frye's apprehension that the "fall of an enemy" is tragic and not comic. "What confusion it is," Olenin reflects. "A man kills another and is happy and satisfied with himself as if he had done something excellent. Can it be that nothing tells him that it is not a reason for any rejoicing, and that happiness lies not in killing, but in sacrificing oneself?" Olenin expresses the essence of the tragic vision revealed to him in the stag's lair.

As a result of his recent revelation in the forest, Olenin is impulsively bent upon doing good. He will test his newly discovered principle of self-sacrificing love. Entertaining the illusion that spiritual regeneration can be achieved overnight, he soon finds an opportunity. Lukashka, although an adept horse thief, aspires to promotion in the cordon by becoming a mounted Cossack. Olenin gives a horse to Lukashka. Perplexed upon receiving the unexpected gift, Lukashka regards Olenin's generosity as a kind of treachery, a Trojan horse, even though the Greeks bring gifts! Though skeptical, Lukashka accepts the gift, and thus becomes a better match for Maryanka. Ironically, for Maryanka's love Olenin is also a competitor. The author's indulgent irony does not, however, impugn the value of self-sacrificing love discovered by Olenin in the stag's lair.

The difficulty critics find in interpreting the author's intent in *The Cossacks* is due in large part to the ambivalent portrayal of Olenin. The complexity of Tolstoy's attitude toward his leading character is evident when we witness Olenin relinquishing both the values of Moscow life and the more immediate claims of the Cossacks, whom he eventually perceives as seriously flawed. Ultimately Tolstoy himself, like Olenin, draws conclusions about the moral values of the Cossacks, especially their propensity to kill.

We have noted that throughout the narrative the author juxtaposes the youthful advocate of war, Lukashka, against the uninitiated exponent of peace, Olenin. In so doing, Tolstoy is not merely drawing contrasts, he is passing value judgments. With this view critics generally agree. The question then arises: What judgments are being made and to whom do they apply?

Numerous critics affirm that Tolstoy's purpose is to portray the Cossacks in a predominantly favorable light, as "natural" men who share the simplicity of their surroundings. Prince Mirsky insists that though the Cossacks are not "good" in the Christian moral sense "the very fact of being natural places them above the distinction of good and evil. The Cossacks kill, fornicate, steal, and still are beautiful in their naturalness, and hopelessly superior to the much more moral, but civilized and consequently contaminated, Olenin."[5]

A similar interpretation is offered by Marc Slonim. "Tolstoy accepts the brutality, and even the cruelty, of the Cossacks, since he admires their naturalness, the unspoiled wholesomeness of their animal existence. This is the Russian version of the Noble Savage. . . ."[6]

More recently a like position has been taken by Isaiah Berlin. "The Cossacks Lukashka or Uncle Yeroshka in *The Cossacks* are morally superior as well as happier and aesthetically more harmonious beings than Olenin. Olenin knows this: indeed that is the heart of the situation."[7]

In some respects views such as these have a good deal to recommend them, for the Cossacks, obeying the laws of nature, enlist our sympathy in many ways. Nevertheless, we must return to the author's insistence upon moral values, especially with regard to war, as affirmed not only in the early sketches but in *War and Peace*, and finally in treatises written as a pacifist, at the close of his career.

The author's attitude at this early stage is succinctly summarized by Hagan, who insists that Tolstoy is suggesting, "in a way of which I am sure he was quite unconscious, that what is admirable in the Cossacks is inseparable from what is also morally offensive. Their freedom from the moral law is the great source of both their enormous attractiveness (for Olenin and Tolstoy alike) and their radical limitations. Tolstoy feels the pull of an ethic of love and self-sacrifice as fully as he feels the pull of an amoral freedom from such an ethic. . . . This is the crux of the whole matter, and the main point about *The Cossacks* is that it expresses this dilemma without ever resolving it."[8]

The author's dilemma is again reflected in the characterization of Maryanka, modeled upon the Solomonide he met in the Caucasus, as his diary of January 7, 1854, reveals. Maryanka is an example of orthodox Christian chastity. Olenin finds her attractive. "Perhaps in her I love nature," he writes in his self-scrutinizing letter. Since Maryanka is intended for Lukashka, Eroshka offers to get Olenin another, "a regular beauty." Olenin is abashed by Eroshka's offer, but Eroshka persists, "God made you and God made the girl too. . . . That's what she was made for; to be loved and to give joy." The old man's view of Natural Law, exempt from the burden of sin, Olenin cannot accept, nor can Maryanka, the only chaste girl in the story.

Nevertheless, John Bayley argues that Tolstoy "strains plausibility in making Maryanka so chaste and severe, towards Lukashka as well as Olenin."[9] Olenin, in Bayley's eyes, is a failure, not only in war but in love—a comical failure compared to the tragic failure of the hero of *The Gipsies*. Pushkin's hero achieves the gipsy girl's love for a time. "But the simple life is also innocently promiscuous: helplessly reverting to the standards of civilization he kills the girl and the gipsy lover with whom he finds her."[10] The rigidity of Tolstoy's moral attitude Bayley finds incongruous. "Olenin, in his enthusiasm for Cossack life, has fallen in love with the one girl who happens not to conform to it."[11] Yet Maryanka is still a Cossack. Of this fact Olenin becomes aware before his departure, when he witnesses the sequel to the ransoming scene—the revenge upon Lukashka.

In the scene, in which the brother of the dead abrek comes to retaliate, Cossacks are killed and Lukashka is critically wounded. But Olenin, who has witnessed fierce fighting as an observer rather than as a participator, returns unscathed to Maryanka. Remembering his proposal of the previous night, he approaches her hopefully, only to find her in tears. She rebuffs him, "Cossacks have been killed," she explains contemptuously. Abruptly Olenin realizes that to become a Cossack it is not enough to live like a Cossack, he must also kill like a Cossack, a commitment he is unable to make.

Nor was Tolstoy ultimately able to make that commitment, although at the time of the writing of *War and Peace* he accepted war as an ironic aspect of human existence. He was convinced that war is inevitable. The conviction that it is man's duty to resist war and to refuse to take part in it came to him later, Maude reminds us. "Yet his inveterate truthfulness, and his personal knowledge of war, caused him to describe it so exactly that the result is tantamount to a condemnation."[12]

The folly and futility of war both Homer and Tolstoy recognize, and express in the mouths of their leading heroes. In the first book of the *Iliad* Achilles confronts Agamemnon with the argument that he has no quarrel with the enemy. "Not by reason of the Trojan spearmen came I hither to fight, for they have not wronged me" (I, 152–153). Likewise, Prince Andrew reminds Pierre, "If no one fought except on his own conviction, there would be no wars." (25)

An opinion near to that held by the author is expressed in *War and Peace* by Prince Andrew on the eve of the battle of Borodino. Reflecting on "the habits of the military," he concludes bitterly, "They meet as we shall meet tomorrow, to murder one another; they kill and maim tens of thousands, and then have thanksgiving services for having killed so many people (they even exaggerate the numbers), and they announce a victory, supposing that the more people they have killed the greater their achievement. How does God above look at them and hear them?" (865)

Unlike the youthful Alanin and Lukashka, Prince Andrew no longer seeks glory in war. But the foolhardiness of the earlier "heroes" foreshadows the folly of Petya Rostov, who seeks a heroism no longer heroic.

Homer understood the poignancy of youthful heroism when he created Polydoros, Priam's son, "the youngest born and the best beloved (XX, 409–410). A youth renowned for fleetness of foot, Polydoros, "in boyish folly, displaying the swiftness of his feet" (XX, 411), is described rushing through the forefront of the fighters until he is slain by Achilles.

Was Tolstoy mindful of Polydoros when he created Petya Rostov? Polydoros is forbidden by his father to fight; Petya, the youngest of the Rostov children, at first forbidden by his parents to fight, joins a regiment and becomes a boy-officer at sixteen.

It is significant that Petya is the only one of the four Rostov children who has no counterpart in life. Nikolay, we recall, is modeled upon Tolstoy's father. The two Rostov girls are modeled, in part, upon members of Tolstoy's wife's family: Natasha upon the author's younger sister-in-law, Tatiana Bers, and Vera upon the older sister-in-law, Liza Bers. But Petya is a figment of the author's imagination.

The final portrayal of Petya, the personification of boyish elan, is the result of gradual development in the author's sketches. At first Petya is not killed in battle. In an early draft the young soldier speaks persistently of his disillusionment and feeling of dissatisfaction with himself. Tolstoy affirms, "This disillusionment and dissatisfaction with oneself is always the stronger, the better the young man is at fighting. Petya was endowed with great ambition, strong nerves and a propensity for blood to flow to his head in such a way that he saw and understood nothing when he was angry. Otherwise he was almost a child. And so he was what is called foolhardy. . . ."[13]

In the definitive edition the disillusionment disappears and Petya is shown in a "constant state of blissful excitement at being grown-up, and in a perpetual ecstatic hurry not to miss any chance to do something really heroic." He is "highly delighted with what he saw and experienced in the army, but at the same time it always seemed to him that the really heroic exploits were being performed just where he did not happen to be. And he was always in a hurry to get where he was not (1161). In the motley company of Denisov's guerrillas, Petya imagines that all his associates are heroes. To him "Denisov was a hero, the esaul a hero, and Tikhon a hero too" (1161).

In the midst of such hardened company Petya hesitates to show pity for a French drummer boy who has been taken captive lest they say, "He's a boy himself and so he pities the boy." But Petya vows, "I'll show them tomorrow whether I'm a boy" (1162). Petya invites the drummer boy into the hut and gives him reassurance, "Don't be afraid, they won't hurt you," as he shyly touches the boy's hand. Now Tolstoy gives a delightful touch to the story as he links the drummer boy with nature. "Vincent, the boy's name, had already been changed by the Cossacks into Vesenny (vernal) and into Vesenya by the peasants and soldiers. In both these adaptations the reference to spring (vesna) matched the impression made by the young lad" (1163). Association of youth with spring brings to mind the simile attributed by Aristotle to Pericles, that the vanishing from their country of the young men who had fallen in war was "as if the spring were taken out of the year."[14]

As prelude to Petya's baptism of fire, on the eve of the raid on the French encampment, a dream removes the youth far from the conflict of war. The dream, releasing a soldier from reality, is used by both Homer and Tolstoy as a psychological nuance which, by relieving tension momentarily, builds to a greater impact. In both epics men in the midst of battle pause to indulge in revery. Thus Hector, before the fatal encounter with Achilles, resolves to stop his flight and face his enemy, but only for a moment. No time now, he reminds himself, to allow his thoughts to wander to a scene remote from the facing of death, to that of a youth and a maiden dallying under oak tree or rock (XXII, 126–128).[15] In like manner Tolstoy's Captain Tushin, in imminent danger, indulges in a revery in which, as an inveterate pipe smoker, he sees the enemy's guns as pipes. "The enemy's guns were in his fancy not guns but pipes from which occasional puffs were blown by an invisible smoker" (205). Also, in the earlier work, *Sevastopol in May,* revery precedes disaster. Here Praskoukin's thoughts turn to a debt left unpaid, a gypsy air, a lady he loved, and a man he had not yet revenged. Yet the thought of death never leaves him, nor the ardent desire to continue living. In all instances the world of fantasy is soon supplanted by a world of crucial action.

Similarly, Petya Rostov enters a world of fantasy, a musical fairyland, on the eve of his fatal adventure. He hears music in his dreams. The music becomes a march of victory. He awakes. The attack on the French begins. Petya, galloping toward the spot where the smoke is thickest, is shot down—a bullet through his head. Thus Tolstoy praises youthful heroism!

In his latter years Tolstoy indicted civilization for allowing war to continue. He now held the opinion that war is an unmitigated evil and that the injunction to vanquish one's enemies is blasphemy. In the stateless society of his imagination he conceived not of a time when the state would become the church and reign over the entire earth, but of an age in which Christian brotherhood would prevail. Although Homer does not envision a time when war will cease, the thought was not foreign to Greek mythmakers. Mythology records the existence of such a utopia, in which self-destructive fratricide yields to the desire of brothers to unite.

It is said that Cadmus, legendary founder of Thebes, having slain the dragon, stood over his conquered foe contemplating its vast size. Presently he heard a voice commanding him to sow the dragon's teeth in the earth. Scarce had he finished the task when the clods began to move and spears, helmets with their nodding plumes, and next the bodies of armed men appeared. Before the eyes of the startled Cadmus, the earthborn brothers began to destroy one another with weapons, until all but five had been slain in mutual strife. Then one of the warriors cast away his weapons and said, "Brothers, let us live in peace!" And on such a beneficent gesture the city of Thebes was founded.

The myth illustrates the belief entertained by Tolstoy in *War and Peace*, that the fittest are not always the most violently aggressive, and that the meek sometimes do inherit the earth. Tolstoy's meek hero Kutuzov forgives the national enemy, the French, "While they were strong we didn't spare ourselves, but now we may even pity them." Prince Andrew forgives his personal enemy, Anatole, before he finds peace in death, and Karataev's Aksyenov before his death forgives his accuser.

The principle animates Natasha in her prayer for the enemy. The priest is praying for victory while Natasha prays for forgiveness of the enemy. The priest invokes the Deity: ". . . smite down our enemies and destroy them swiftly beneath the feet of Thy faithful servants! For Thou are the defense, the succor, and the victory of them that put their trust in Thee." Natasha, on the other hand, "could not pray that her enemies might be trampled under foot when but a few minutes before she had been wishing she had more of them that she might pray for them." Natasha prays to God "to forgive them all, and her too, and to give them all, and her too, peace and happiness." Tolstoy concludes, "And it seemed to her that God heard her prayer" (735–736).

When Tolstoy noted all that was done by men who professed Christianity, and particularly by priests who went as chaplains to teach soldiers Christian principles without teaching them it is wrong to fight, he was horrified. To condone war seemed to him the antithesis of every Christian tenet. Because he could not subordinate the truth to the authority of the Church, he was "excommunicated," though it should be mentioned that the edict was not a formal excommunication since it was not couched in canonical language.[16]

When Tolstoy died, unreconciled to the Orthodox Church, the Holy Synod forbade priests to perform the last rites. Ironically, the Church was conforming to the author's wishes, for two years before his death he had dictated to his secretary his desire that no ceremonies be performed at his funeral. "A wooden coffin, and whoever wishes, carry it or cart it to Zakas, opposite the ravine at the place of the 'green stick.' At least there's a reason for selecting that and no other place." For hours mourners entered the house and filed by the open coffin, which was later closed and carried by the author's sons to the woods nearby. No priests were present at this first public funeral in Russia without religious rites.

144

Tolstoy was buried in the spot he had selected, by the road at the edge of a ravine in the Zakas woods, where his beloved brother Nikolai, when they were children, declared he had hidden the little green stick, on which was written the wonderful secret which when known to mankind would make all men happy. All evil would vanish from the earth and, as in the childhood fantasy, all men would love one another and become brothers.[17] At the close of his life Tolstoy, so intent upon creating heroes who embodied the precepts of Christ, became, without benefit of clergy, a Christlike hero to his admirers.

"To create is to live again" Camus says of Proust in *Le Mythe de Sisyphe*. In a deeper sense it might be said that Tolstoy the creator became his creations—Prince Andrew, Pierre, Kutuzov, Karataev—reincarnate in a new myth of the Christian hero.

Notes

NOTES

THE Norton Critical Edition of *War and Peace* (based upon the Maude translation) edited by George Gibian is the source of references in the text as well as references to essays in criticism from Russian sources unless otherwise indicated.

References to the *Iliad* will be found in the Loeb Edition, though the translations, unless otherwise indicated, are from the translation of Lang, Leaf, and Myers, in the Modern Library Edition.

PREFACE

1. The quotation illustrates Callimachus' epigrammatic way of denigrating long works, especially epic. Callimachus' view was opposed by Apollonius of Rhodes, whose *Argonautica* was an answer to the former's claim that the age was unsuited for epic.

CHAPTER I

1. Werner Jaeger, *Paideia: The Ideals of Greek Culture* (New York: Oxford University Press, 1945), I, 40. Translated by Gilbert Highet. Second Edition.
2. See also *Odyssey*, VII, 254–366, 487–520; XIII, 27–28.
3. A. B. Lord, "Homer and Other Epic Poetry," in *A Companion to Homer* (London: Macmillan & Co., Ltd., 1962), pp. 181–183. Edited by Alan J. P. Wace and Frank H. Stubbings.
4. *Ibid.*, pp. 205–211.
5. *Odyssey* (Oxford: Clarendon Press, 1916), Note to XIX, 163. A flood myth, similar to that of Noah's Ark, relates that a

pious old couple are the sole survivors of a deluge. After the flood they are duty-bound to repeople the earth. Consulting an oracle, they are told, "Cast behind you the bones of your mother." Obeying the injunction, they cast over their shoulders the stones of the earth, whence issue a new race—but ever since that time men have been stony of heart. To such a race Penelope does not attribute her origin.

6. Herodotus, II, 116–117.

7. J. A. Davison, "The Homeric Question," in *A Companion to Homer*, pp. 234–265.

8. Hesiod, *Works and Days*, pp. 156–174, *passim*. William Chase Green, *Moira: Good and Evil in Greek Thought* (Cambridge, Mass.: Harvard University Press, 1948), p. 32.

9. Maurice (C. M.) Bowra, "Style," in *A Companion to Homer*, p. 36.

10. A further question remains. How did the Homeric poems reach mainland Greece, and subsequently the entire Western world, from Ionia? One view maintains that Hipparchus, son of the tyrant Peisistratus, was the first to bring them to Attica. We are told that Hipparchus, who made a Poets' Circle, brought Homer's work to Athens and ordained that in the Panathenaic competition the rhapsodes should follow one another in reciting the poems, and they were to deliver the lines in their proper continuity to the end. Such a rule would demand a definitive version, but that the Peisistratidae were the first to produce a written text of Homer, anticipating the Ionians, is doubtful. Plato, *Hipparchus*, 228 B. See also Lilian H. Jeffery, "Writing," in *A Companion to Homer*, p. 558.

11. Georg Lukacs, *Studies in European Realism* (New York: Grosset & Dunlap, c. 1964), p. 149.

12. Letter to M. About, editor of *Le XIXe Siecle*, January 20, 1880. Norton Edition, p. 1388.

13. Northrop Frye, *Anatomy of Criticism* (New York: Atheneum, 1966), pp. 247–248.

14. Jubilee Edition, XIII, 53.

15. Letter to M. N. Katkov, January 3, 1865. Jubilee Edition, LX1, 67.

16. Jubilee Edition, XLVIII, 64.

17. A. B. Goldenweiser, *Vblizi Tolstogo* (Moscow-Leningrad, 1959), p. 113.

18. M. Gorky, *Reminiscences of Tolstoy, Chekhov, and Andreev* (New York: Dover Publications, 1948), p. 57.

19. Paul Birukoff, *Leo Tolstoy: Childhood and Youth* (New York: C. Scribner's Sons, 1911), p. 200. Compiled by Paul Birukoff and revised by Leo Tolstoy. Translated from the Russian.

20. Aylmer Maude lived in Russia for more than twenty-three years. He and his wife, Louise Maude, who was born in Moscow and lived there the first forty years of her life, were disciples of Tolstoy. They collaborated in selecting the best text of *War and Peace* and translating it with remarkable accuracy.

21. Aylmer Maude, *The Life of Tolstoy: First Fifty Years* (London: Constable, 1908), I, 172.

22. Ernest J. Simmons, *Leo Tolstoy* (Boston: Little, Brown & Co., 1946), p. 160.

23. Birukoff, p. 248.

24. *L. N. Tolstoj, Sobranie Socinenij*, 20 volumes (Moskva, 1960–1965), XIX. *The Private Diary of Leo Tolstoy 1853–1857* (London: William Heinemann, Ltd., 1927). Edited by Aylmer Maude. Translated by Louise and Aylmer Maude. Reprint (New York: Kraus Reprint Co., 1972). The following entries refer to the *Iliad:* August 15, 16, 17, 24, 29, in the year 1857.

25. Simmons, *Leo Tolstoy*, p. 224 n.

26. Leo Tolstoy, *What Is Art?* (New York: Bobbs-Merrill Co., Inc., c. 1960), p. 97. Translated by Aylmer Maude.

27. Leo Wiener, *The Complete Works of Count Tolstoy* (Boston: D. Estes & Co., 1904–1905), IV, 271–272. Translated from the Russian and edited by Leo Wiener.

28. Isaiah Berlin, "Tolstoy and Enlightenment," *Encounter*, XVI, No. 2 (February 1961), 36.
29. Simmons, *Leo Tolstoy*, p. 258.
30. *Ibid.*, p. 289.
31. Maude, *Life*, I, 327.
32. *Ibid.*, I, 328.
33. Ernest J. Simmons, *Introduction to Tolstoy's Writings* (Chicago: University of Chicago Press, 1968), p. 154.
34. Maude, *Life*, I, 333.
35. Simmons, *Leo Tolstoy*, p. 289.
36. *Ibid.*, p. 274. Cf. S. A. Tolstaya, "Avtobiografiya," *Nachala* (1926), p. 1.
37. Simmons, *Leo Tolstoy*, p. 284.
38. Maude, *Life*, I, 328–329.
39. *What Is Art?* p. 144.
40. Maude, *The Life of Tolstoy: Later Years*, II, 544.
41. Jaeger, I, 6.
42. A fuller account of these years may be found in the preface to the *Diary 1853–1857*.
43. The Decembrists were a secret society of officers and gentlemen who had brought back from Russia's victorious campaign in Europe the new ideal of political enlightenment, particularly as found in France. They failed in their *coup d'etat* to secure the accession of Alexander I's brother Constantine and the granting of a constitution for Russia. Many of the soldiers who cheered "Constantine and Constitution" were executed by Nicholas II or exiled to Siberia. Pushkin always said he would have taken part had he been in Petersburg at the time.
44. Draft for an Introduction to *War and Peace*, Draft 2. Norton Edition, p. 1364.
45. *Idem.*
46. Simmons, *Leo Tolsoy*, p. 270.
47. Letter to L. I. Volkonskaya, May 3, 1865. Norton Edition, 1359.
48. Simmons, *Leo Tolstoy*, p. 267.

CHAPTER II

1. Jaeger, I, 3–29, *passim.*
2. *Ibid.*, I, 26.
3. *Nicomachean Ethics,* IX, 8. Jaeger, I, 12.
4. *Ibid.*, IX, 8, 1168 b 27.
5. *Ibid.*, IX, 8, 1169 z 18 ff.
6. Jaeger, I, 4 and 416 n 4.
7. Translation according to Jaeger, I, 10–11.
8. *Ibid.*, I, 8.
9. *Nicomachean Ethics,* I, 5, 1095 b 26.
10. See also XVIII, 95–97; XVIII, 440–441.
11. Letter to P. I. Bartenev, August 16–18, 1867. Norton Edition, p. 1361. The episode is found in *War and Peace,* Book VIII, Chapters 17–21.
12. Frye, p. 219.
13. John Hagan, "On the Craftsmanship of *War and Peace*," *Slavic and East European Journal,* XIII, No. 2 (Summer 1969), 181.
14. Peritonitis is followed by gangrene. Norton Edition, p. 1021 n, Maude remarks: "The advance of science has added many terrors to war, but the introduction of antiseptic surgery has removed one of the worst horrors of former times. As A. Chekhov—a doctor as well as a writer—remarked: that an officer of Prince Andrew's position should suffer and die from gangrene which he, Chekhov, could have prevented, is a striking example of the deplorable state of medical knowledge in 1812."
15. Once earlier, in recalling Natasha, Andrew understood that it was "that very soul of hers which seemed to be fettered by her body" which he loved (867).
16. Simmons, *Introduction to Tolstoy's Writings,* p. 76. Like Christ, the short-lived hero, Prince Andrew lives thirty-three years.
17. Comparable is the detachment from life of Platon Karataev (1078). "Karataev had no attachments, friendships, or love,

as Pierre understood them, but loved and lived affectionately with everything life brought him in contact with, particularly with man—not any particular man, but those with whom he happened to be. He loved his dog, his comrades, the French, and Pierre who was his neighbor, but Pierre felt that in spite of Karataev's affectionate tenderness for him . . . he would not have grieved for a moment at parting from him."

18. Maude, *Life*, I, 424. On the other hand, Simmons (*Introduction to Tolstoy's Writings*, p. 78) finds that even in negative characters Tolstoy almost always discovers some good. The reprehensible Dolohov is devoted to his mother and the obnoxious Anatole is apparently brave in combat.

19. Jaeger, I, 42. Thersites (II, 212–222) is the only character in the *Iliad* who receives detailed physical description and he is described at length precisely because he varies from the standard of the hero. Dolon (X, 314–316) is described briefly as ill-favored to look upon, but we note he is admirably "swift of foot." The burden of Thersites' tirade against Agamemnon is that Agamemnon is deriving the benefit from the war while the other soldiers bear its hardships. One recalls that Achilles, though in wrath, had made a similar accusation against Agamemnon, saying, "When the apportioning cometh then is thy meed far ampler" (when compared to his own). (I, 166).

20. Letter to M. S. Bashilov, April 4 and December 1, 1866; February 28, 1867. Norton Edition, p. 1360. Helene also has a "marble brow" (344).

21. A few years later, while Tolstoy was writing *Anna Karenina*, *La Belle Helene*, a comic opera in three acts, with music by Offenbach, was in vogue in Moscow and Petersburg. The opera tells of the judgment of Paris and the subsequent abduction of Helen by Paris during the absence of Menelaus. In *Anna Karenina* Karenin is thinking of instances of the unfaithfulness of wives, beginning with La Belle Helene. Norton Edition of *Anna Karenina*, p. 255 n.

NOTES

CHAPTER III

1. Draft for an Introduction to *War and Peace*, Draft I, Norton Edition, p. 1363.
2. *Poetics*, 1460 a 18–19. Translated by S. H. Butcher.
3. Thucydides, *The History of the Peloponnesian War*, I, 21.
4. Herodotus, II, 113–118.
5. *Ibid.*, II, 23, 120.
6. *Ibid.*, II, 113.
7. *Ibid.*, II, 114.
8. *Idem.*
9. *Poetics*, 1451 a 36–b 9.
10. *Ibid.*, 1461 b 11–12. Cf. 1460 a 26–27.
11. N. N. Strakhov, *Kriticheskie stati ob I. S. Turgeneve i. L. N. Tolstom* (St. Petersburg, 1895), pp. 352–361, *passim.* Translated by George Gibian, Norton Edition, p. 1386.
12. *Ibid.* Norton Edition, p. 1385.
13. *Ibid.* Norton Edition, p. 1382.
14. *Ibid.* Norton Edition, p. 1387.
15. C. M. Bowra, *Heroic Poetry* (London: Macmillan & Co., Ltd., 1952), p. 113.
16. Strakhov, pp. 352–361, *passim.* Norton Edition, p. 1385.
17. Norton Edition, p. 16 n.
18. Isaiah Berlin, "Lev Tolstoy's Historical Scepticism," *Oxford Slavonic Papers*, II (1951), 33. The expanded article became a monograph entitled *The Hedgehog and the Fox* (London, 1955). Norton Edition, p. 1446 n.
19. *Odyssey*, I, 34.
20. Frye, p. 210.
21. See also *Odyssey*, I, 35–43; III, 248–310; IV, 512–537; XI, 397–454).
22. Greene, pp. 15–16. The urns of Zeus like the scales of Zeus (VIII, 69–72; XVI, 658; XIX, 223–224) are probably traditional in origin. Images of the urns and the spinning of Fate (and of the gods) (XX, 127–128; XXIV, 209–210; XXIV, 525) seem to be traditional formulae to express the role of fate or

of the gods, and the use of one or the other may be determined in a given instance by the exigencies of oral versification.

23. The Greek admits of the rendering "two urns . . . of the evil gifts that he giveth, and one of blessings," but the rendering given here agrees with Plato's interpretation (*Republic*, II, 379 D).

24. Greene, p. 48.

25. Paul Debreczeny, "Freedom and Necessity: A Reconsideration of *War and Peace*," *Papers on Language and Literature*, VII, No. 2 (Spring 1971), 185–198.

26. Boris Eikhenbaum, "Tolstoy's Essays as an Element of Structure," from *Lev Tolstoy: Kniga vtoraya, 60ye gody*, pp. 375–378. Translated by George Gibian. Norton Edition, p. 1444.

27. R. F. Christian, *Tolstoy's "War and Peace"* (Oxford: Clarendon Press, 1962), p. 146.

28. Maude, *Life*, I, 427.

29. Bowra, "Composition," in *A Companion to Homer*, p. 58.

30. *Ibid.*, p. 43.

31. *Poetics*, 1462 b 11.

32. Joyce was interested in the cyclical theory of history as enunciated by Giambattista Vico—that the course of history runs in the rhythm of *corso* and *ricorso*. Vico's doctrine underlies the recurrence—the eternal return—theme of *Finnegans Wake*.

33. A similar "mysterious power" appears in two other episodes. That "mysterious, callous force which compelled people against their will to kill their fellow men" (1125), the effect of which Pierre had witnessed during the execution (at which he had been unexpectedly reprieved) appears again in the prison camp when French officers, against their will, obey the command to shoot those who cannot keep pace on the march. Platon Karataev is one of the victims.

34. Berlin, "Lev Tolstoy's Historical Scepticism," p. 40.

35. Norton Edition, 1078 n. Karataev's pronunciation of "Christian" identifies the word with "peasant," since the pronunciation in Russian is very similar.
36. Christian, pp. 41–45.
37. Norton Edition, p. 1178 n.
38. Leo Tolstoy, *Anna Karenina* (New York: W. W. Norton & Co., Inc., 1970). Translated by George Gibian. Norton Edition, p. 793, also p. 789 n. Dostoevsky's comments were published in 1877 in his magazine *Diary of a Writer*. Dostoevsky's words recall the many submissive characters in *War and Peace*—those who refuse to judge. Princess Mary is a leading example.
39. Birukoff, p. 248. Maude, *Life*, I, 172, states it this way: "At this time he read (in translation) the *Iliad* and the Gospels, which both impressed him greatly. 'I have finished reading the indescribably beautiful end of the *Iliad*,' he notes, and expresses his regret that there is no connection between those two wonderful works." The author's Diary of August 29, 1857, reads, "After the *Iliad* read the Gospels, which I have not done for a long time. How could Homer not know that goodness is love!"
40. Frye, p. 319.
41. Greene, p. 48. There were cults of Reverence (*Aidos*) and of Pity (*Eleos*) in Athens at one time.
42. Xenophanes, Fragment, 17, 30.
43. Bowra, *Heroic Poetry*, p. 68.
44. Wiener, *The Complete Works of Count Tolstoy*, IV, 297.
45. Anton Chekhov to A. S. Suverin, March 27, 1894, in *A Treasury of Classic Russian Literature* (New York: Capricorn Books, 1943) p. 78. Edited by John Cournos.

NOTES

CHAPTER IV

1. Frye, p. 17.
2. Milman Parry, "Studies in the Epic Technique of Oral Verse-Making," *Harvard Studies in Classical Philology*, XLIII, (1932), 14.
3. *Ibid.*, p. 73.
4. Bowra, "Style," in *A Companion to Homer*, p. 29.
5. Parry, p. 81.
6. Norton Edition, p. 1305 n.
7. Christian, pp. 148–149.
8. *Rhetoric*, 1412 a 7–10.
9. The term *ostranenie* was coined by Shklovsky in the essay "Art as Device" (*Iskusstvo kak priem*, 1917). For a fuller explanation, see *Dnevnik molodosti L'va Nikolaievicha Tolstogo* (The Diary of Youth of Lev Nikolaievich Tolstoi) (Moscow, 1917), pp. 30–31. First edition. Edited by V. G. Chertkov.
10. *Rhetoric*, 1406 b.
11. *Poetics*, 1459 a 6–8.
12. For a fuller discussion of Tolstoy's imagery see the article by James M. Curtis, "The Function of Imagery in *War and Peace*," *Slavic Review*, XXIX, No. 3, (September 1970), 460–480.
13. George M. Calhoun, "Polity and Society," in *A Companion to Homer*, p. 462.
14. Bowra, "Composition," in *A Companion to Homer*, p. 70.
15. Christian, p. 164. *Iliad*, II, 87–93.
16. The Greeks, too, had a word for it, as the maxim of the unknown author in the Greek Anthology indicates.

Σκηνὴ πᾶς ὁ βίος καὶ παίγνιον
All life is a stage, a play.

17. John Hagan discovers that each of the five protagonists in *War and Peace* is engaged in a moral quest, and that

Andrew pursues his quest through five distinct cycles of death and rebirth. John Hagan, "A Pattern of Character Development in *War and Peace:* Prince Andrej," *Slavic and East European Journal,* XIII, No. 2 (Summer 1969), 164–190.

18. In a lighter vein, one might mention the round ring of tobacco smoke which perfectly embodies Berg's dream of happiness (489) and the round biscuits thrown by the Emperor to the crowd gathered in the Kremlin courtyard. Petya catches one of the biscuits and decides to join the army (749–750).

19. In *Sevastopol in May* a little girl mistakes the bombs for stars. "The stars, the stars, look how they roll. . . ."

20. Christian, p. 76.

21. Cf. Gaston Bachelard, "The Phenomenology of Roundness," in *European Literary Theory and Practice: From Existential Phenomenology to Structuralism* (New York: Delta Publishing Co., Inc., (1973), pp. 263–271. Edited and with an introduction by Vernon W. Gras.

22. Carl G. Jung, *Man and His Symbols* (Garden City, N.Y.: Doubleday & Co., Inc., 1964), pp. 218–219.

CHAPTER V

1. In 1862, to satisfy a thousand-ruble gambling debt, Tolstoy secured an advance from the publisher, M. N. Katkov, and after final revision the first part appeared in *The Russian Herald* in 1863. Compare Boris Eikhenbaum, *The Young Tolstoi* (Ann Arbor, Michigan: Ardis, c. 1972), p. 98 n. Translation edited by Gary Kern.

2. John Hagan, "Ambivalence in Tolstoy's *The Cossacks*," *Novel*, III, No. 1 (Fall 1969), 34.

3. Leo Tolstoy, *The Cossacks* and *The Raid* (New York: The New American Library of World Literature, Inc., 1961). Afterword by F. D. Reeve, p. 218.

4. Hagan, "Ambivalence in Tolstoy's *The Cossacks*," *Novel*, p. 41.

5. D. S. Mirsky, *A History of Russian Literature*. Abridged by Francis J. Whitfield (New York, A. A. Knopf, 1949), p. 257.

6. Marc Slonim, *The Epic of Russian Literature* (New York: Oxford University Press, 1950), p. 314.

7. Isaiah Berlin, "Tolstoy and Enlightenment," *Tolstoy, A Collection of Critical Essays*. Edited by Ralph E. Matlaw (Englewood Cliffs, New Jersey, 1967), pp. 37–38. For similar interpretations see Edward A. Steiner, *Tolstoy, The Man and His Message* (New York, 1908), p. 71; Janko Lavrin, *Tolstoy, An Approach* (New York, 1946), p. 73; and Marcelle Ehrhard, *Russian Literature* (New York, 1963), p. 88. Translated by Philip Minto.

8. Hagan, "Ambivalence in Tolstoy's *The Cossacks*," *Novel*, p. 42.

9. John Bayley, *Tolstoy and the Novel* (New York: Viking Press, Inc., 1968), p. 272.

10. *Idem.*

11. *Ibid.*, p. 273.

12. Maude, *Life*, I, 426.

13. Christian, p. 27.

14. *Rhetoric*, 1411 a 25.

15. The Loeb translation reads: "In no wise may I now from oak-tree or from rock hold dalliance with him, even as youth

and maiden—youth and maiden!—hold dalliance one with the other." "The repetition of the phrase seems best understood as intended to mark the grim contrast between the real and the imagined situation." Loeb Edition, II, 463 n.

16. Simmons, *Leo Tolstoy,* p. 595.
17. *Ibid.,* p. 774.

Index

INDEX
of Names and Subjects

INDEX

Catherine II (the Great), 28, 91.

"Caucasian Sketches" by Tolstoy, 131.

Caucasus, 23, 125–128, 131.

Chanson de Roland, 97.

Chaos, 10.

Chiron, 32.

Chechen, 128, 132, 134.

Chekhov, A., 99, 153 n 14, 157 n 45.

Childhood, 23, 25.

Childlike intuition, 121–123.

Christ, iv, 10, 31, 67, 123.

Christian, R. F., 78, 107, 113, 156 n 27, 157 n 36, 158 n 7, 15; 159 n 20, 160 n 13.

Christianity, 10, 34, 98.

Clytemnestra, 90.

Companion to Homer, A, 156 n 29, 30; 158 n 4, 13, 14.

Compassion (cf. *eleos*), 49, 82, 95–98.

Complete Works of Count Tolstoy, The, (L. Wiener), 151 n 27, 157 n 44.

"Composition" by C. M. Bowra, 156 n 29, 30; 158 n 14.

Confession, A., 49, 53, 83, 99.

Constantine (brother of Alexander I), 152 n 43.

Contemporary, The, 23, 126.

Cosmos, 8.

Cossack, 128, 129, 131, 136–138, 141.

Cossacks, The, 23, 24, 127, 128, 131, 134–137, 160 n 3.

Courage (ideal of Greek culture), 21.

Crashaw, R., 123.

Crimean War, 15, 23.

Curtis, J. M., 158 n 12.

Daimon, 7.

Dante, 124.

David (Old Testament king), 45, 73.

Davison, J. A., 150 n 7.

Death, 7–11, 43, 45, 51–53, 75.

Debreczeny, P., 77, 156 n 25.

Decay, 9.

Decembrists, 26, 152 n 43; Hero, 25; Decembrist Revolt of 1825, 25.

Demodocus, 6, 79.

Denisov, V. D., 141.

Deucalion, vi.

"The Devil" by Tolstoy, 19.

Diary of a Writer by Dostoevsky, 157 n 38.

Dike (justice), 8.

Dio of Prusa, 54, 55.

Diomedes, 36, 79, 127.

Dionysus, 115.

Dnevnik molodosti L'va Nikolaievicha Tolstogo, 158 n 9.

Dokhturov, General, 69.

Dolohov, F. I., 54, 57, 58, 154 n 18.

INDEX

INDEX

INDEX

INDEX
of Greek and Russian
Words and Phrases

Greek words which have been transliterated appear in the Index of Names and Subjects. Russian words listed below have been transliterated.

Greek:

ἀγαθὴ δὲ παραίφασίς ἐστιν ἑταίρον, 105.

ἀγαθός, 22.

αἰὲν ἀριστεύειν καὶ ὑπείροχον ἔμμεναι ἄλλων, 36.

αἴσιμον ἦμαρ, 74.

ἀρεταί, 103.

ἀρχή, 15.

δῖος, 22.

ἐνέργεια, 109.

ἦθος ἀνθρώπῳ δαίμον, 76.

θεὰ γλαυκῶπις Ἀθήνη, 107.

κλέα ἀνδρῶν, 6, 90.

Μέγα βιβλίον, μέγα κακόν (Callimachus), vii.

μεγάθυμος Ἀχιλλεύς, 107.

177

INDEX

μοῖρα, 74.

οὐ γὰρ ἀπὸ δρυός ἐσσι παλαιφάτου οὐδ᾽ ἀπὸ πέτρης, 8

πόδας ὠκὺς Ἀχιλλεύς, 107.

πολύμητις, 108.

ῥεχθὲν δέ τε νήπιος ἔγνω, 105.

Σκηνὴ πᾶς ὁ βίος καὶ παίγνιον, 158 n 16.

ὑπὲρ μόρον, 75.

φιλαυτία, 33.

Russian:

krugly (round), 119, 120.

mir (world; peace), 124.

narod (people), 84.

REGISTER OF DATES